Adults learning languages

Also available from CILT, the National Centre for Languages:

DIY techniques for language learners
María Fernández-Toro and Francis R Jones

European Language Portfolio for Adult and Vocational Purposes

Language learning for work in a multilingual world
Ed. Cherry Sewell

CILT, the National Centre for Languages, seeks to support and develop multilingualism and intercultural competence among all sectors of the population in the UK.

CILT serves education, business and the wider community with:
• specialised and impartial information services;
• high quality advice and professional development;
• expert support for innovation and development;
• quality improvement in language skills and service provision.

CILT is a charitable trust, supported by the DfES and other Government departments throughout the UK.

Adults learning languages

A CILT guide to good practice

Edited by Henriette Harnisch
& Pauline Swanton

The views expressed in this publication are the editors' and contributors' and do not necessarily represent those of CILT, the National Centre for Languages.

First published 2004 by CILT, the National Centre for Languages, 20 Bedfordbury, London WC2N 4LB.

Copyright © CILT, the National Centre for Languages 2004.

Cover photography © 2003, Barbara Ludman/iwitness. Illustrations on p82 by Richard Duszczak.

ISBN 1 904243 08 8

A catalogue record for this book is available from the British Library.

Printed in Great Britain by Hobbs.

CILT Publications are available from: **Central Books**, 99 Wallis Rd, London E9 5LN. Tel: 0845 458 9910. Fax: 0845 458 9912. Book trade representation (UK and Ireland): **Broadcast Book Services**, Charter House, 29a London Rd, Croydon CR0 2RE. Tel: 020 8681 8949. Fax: 020 8688 0615.

Contents

Languages: a minority pursuit or a national priority?

■ Alan Moys

While the title of this book indicates clearly that it is of specialist interest, it has two quite distinct potential readerships. It will be essential reading for existing teachers of languages to adults, for whom professional development is an increasingly important element of their work if they are to keep abreast of current thinking. At the same time, *Adults learning languages* provides a rich vein of advice and inspiration for anyone entering – or thinking of entering – the world of adult learning as a languages tutor. These two readership groups, while sharing an interest in and enthusiasm for languages, will nonetheless have distinct needs which this publication seeks to meet. In particular, many new teachers of languages to adults are native speakers of the language they wish to teach – and will be looking for guidance, not only about methods and approaches, but also about the learners themselves and about the broader educational, cultural and political context of the teacher's task. As it happens, the context is undergoing major changes in these opening years of the 21st century, so it seems logical in this preface to look at these important background issues. Hence my question, Languages: a minority pursuit or a national priority?

It would be all too easy to dismiss language learning as no more than an optional extra in a country whose language has rapidly achieved the status of a global 'lingua franca'. The report of the Nuffield Languages Inquiry, published in 2000, while fully acknowledging the global role of English, warned however that:

> '... the UK's complacent view of its limited capacity in other languages is understandable. It is also dangerous. In a world where bilingualism and plurilingualism are commonplace, monolingualism implies inflexibility, insensitivity and arrogance. Much that is essential to our society, its health and its interests – including effective choice in policy, realisation of citizenship, effective overseas links and openness to the inventions of other cultures – will not be achieved in one language alone.' (Languages: the next generation, the Nuffield Foundation, 2000).

Indeed, the effects of globalisation in business, alongside increasingly accessible world travel and ever cheaper international communication by telephone, the media, e-mail and the Internet, serve to underline the force of this argument. A variety of opinion polls and surveys in the UK have revealed a public which is increasingly convinced of the importance of language learning, and press coverage and support have been generous in recent years. One of the most powerful endorsements came from no less than the Chairman of the English-Speaking Union, Lord Watson, who reminded us that:

> 'It is our good fortune and our real advantage that, in an age of globalisation, English has become a global language. But if we use that as an excuse to allow our own foreign language abilities to wither away, if we do not have a strategic and national action to reverse the decline, an extraordinary irony will emerge: that in a world which speaks our language we will be increasingly isolated; that in an integrating continent we will become more insular; and that in a global village we will be choosing to live on our own. I hope that we will not be confronted with that irony.'

Happily, the signs are that the argument that 'English is not enough' is being won. In 2002, the Government published its long-awaited national strategy for languages, declaring that:

> '... in the knowledge society of the 21st century, language competence and international understanding are not optional extras, they are an essential part of being a citizen.'

... and concluding that we must therefore:

> '... transform our national capacity in languages.' (*Languages for all: languages for life. A strategy for England.* Department for Education and Skills, 2002).

The central plank of the Strategy is to provide all children with an entitlement to learn another language from age seven by the year 2010, and the remainder of the document focuses principally on the schools sector and on employment, with only a brief section on adult learning. There has been justifiable criticism of this imbalance, which sits uncomfortably with the declared vision of transforming our national capability. At the same time, we must not underestimate the importance of the Government's initiative. A world figure in the field of language policy, Jo lo Bianco, reminds us that:

> 'Once public authorities make declarations of the kind set out in the Strategy, they open themselves to scrutiny, to evaluation of what they claim, to criticism: they have raised public expectation and have validated public agitation for better language planning and enhanced provision.'

In this context, the adult learning sector has a powerful case to make, and the national and local Learning and Skills Councils have a responsibility to reflect government policy in their planning. The national languages strategy also proposes to introduce a new user-friendly national system for recognising learner achievement in languages at all levels (see Appendix, p134) – a plan which will be welcomed equally in the field of adult learning.

One of the striking (and often controversial) features of public policy debate today is the increasing presence of 'the market' in the vocabulary, and by any measure adult learning is very strongly placed when we consider the 'demand' side of any strategy for national capability in languages. On the one hand, the existing market for adult language learning remains buoyant in spite of decades of neglect by central government, and has been further strengthened by the exciting new mechanisms for learning through the Internet and the personal computer. In addition, new potential audiences for language learning are opening up as a result of policy decisions and patterns of learning elsewhere in the education system. In higher education, we have seen a huge increase in the numbers of students studying a language as a practical skill alongside other disciplines. As they move on from full time education, these graduates will in many cases want to continue or renew their language skills, either for personal or professional reasons, and many will look to their local adult education service to provide this facility. Another new market is likely to arise from the Government's decision to make languages optional in secondary schools from age 14, a move which will lead to many young people abandoning languages prematurely, only to find later that they need to get back on the language-learning ladder. Adult learning in this case can provide a dual benefit, not just in terms of recovering lost ground. Alwena Lamping cogently reminds us of the importance of adults as role models, in her articles and in one of the findings of the Nuffield Languages Inquiry:

> *'Adults with language skills...are more likely to display tolerance and intercultural understanding. They communicate these values, along with their enthusiasm for languages, to their children – and progress in schools depends as much on parental attitudes as on educational policy.'*

Government will do well to take seriously this reminder that positive action in adult education can have a direct bearing on the success of the National Strategy in schools.

The adult language-learning field remains one of stimulating diversity: learners of all ages and backgrounds, bringing a whole range of previous experience to bear on their learning, driven by personal or professional motivations, drawing satisfaction from achievements at all levels, and equipping themselves better for life as global citizens. A minority pursuit or a national priority? Teaching to such objectives is a noble cause, and the contributors to this latest CILT publication greatly enrich the process.

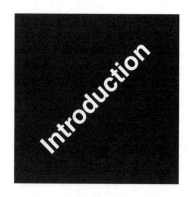

Aims, audience and approach

■ Henriette Harnisch & Pauline Swanton

Background

In 1992 CILT published *The adult language learner*. This was essentially a manual of information and guidance for adult tutors of languages giving ideas and inspiration that would help them to meet the then anticipated increase in demand for language tuition.

If the numbers of new learners, as a result of the Single European Market, failed to live up to expectation, the success and efficacy of the book did not disappoint. Ten years on it continued to be critical reading for those contemplating entering and already part of the world of adult language teaching and learning. The backbone of many a training course, friend and ally of the isolated tutor, the source of ideas, reassurance and valuable insights, the book quickly established itself as a seminal text.

Adult education, however, never stands still. In a decade that has seen funding changes, a higher profile for lifelong learning, the political desire to widen participation, the birth of the Adult Learning Inspectorate and the launch of a national languages strategy, language teachers are challenged, as never before, in their work. *Adults learning languages* intends to provide teachers and managers with the information and tools to rise to the challenge.

Since the publication of *The adult language learner* activity has focused essentially on raising the profile of language learning in the UK. This, in turn, has led to consideration of strategies for securing effective international participation for those with a mother tongue that has gone global. The debate has permitted a certain amount of celebration of the achievement of adult education so far, but has also raised questions about the nature of the work and the profile of the learners. It is time, therefore, to revisit the issues of adult education and to assess their impact on language teaching and learning. *Adults learning languages* undertakes to do just that – in the context of today's changing expectations and requirements.

Aims

As the spotlight falls increasingly on the quality of the education that is offered, it is important that teachers of languages to adults should acquire both the tools of the trade and a general understanding of the sector within which they operate. *Adults learning languages* seeks to provide practical assistance for teachers by offering examples from languages classrooms, by debating pedagogy and methodology, and by explaining the context within which teachers are required to work.

Isolation remains a fact of life for many adult language teachers. There is still a patchy approach to their support and development, and poor infrastructures militate against the sharing and implementation of good practice. Our aspiration in this book, therefore, is to give an overview of the skills, knowledge and understanding that underpin competent teacher performance. Contributors raise key aspects of teaching languages to adults and they propose responses to the various emphases from learners, funders and quality controllers.

One of the many attributes of the successful adult educator is a high degree of creativity and flexibility. Prescription, therefore, is not an intention of the book. It is anticipated that the messages contained in it will be subject to debate and that teachers and prospective teachers will continue to take advantage of the fact that truly innovative work still can and should be part of their brief.

Which languages?

The luxury of having to define the range of languages to be covered is something that is peculiar to the education of adults, as opposed to children, in the UK. The scope for learning tends to be wider in adult education programmes than elsewhere and may include a regular menu of French, German, Spanish, Italian plus the more exotic European options, languages from further afield, notably the Pacific Rim, the Middle East and South East Asia, as well as the classics. In addition, community languages are well represented, particularly in areas of high mixed ethnicity, and it is not unusual to find that British Sign Language and English as a Foreign Language are included in the offer to mature learners.

Our contributors offer advice that is based on their experiences of teaching another 'live' language to a predominantly English-speaking audience. We do not deal with issues of improving mother tongue aptitude (in the area of community languages, for example), nor do we address the different motivations of those who are learning English as a Foreign Language. The complex political and cultural aspects of languages that co-exist with English in the UK (community and British sign language, for example) would take the discussion beyond the scope of this book.

Target audiences

The teaching of adults takes place in a very wide range of institutions, services and venues. The teacher of adults may be employed by a Local Education Authority, by a College of Further Education, by a higher education establishment, by a voluntary or charitable organisation, by a self-help educational foundation – the list is lengthy.

Historically, teachers have been divided by sector – Further Education, Adult Education (generally indicating Local Education Authority provision) or Continuing Education. This is not particularly helpful as across all of these sectors the profile of the teacher of adults and the nature of his or her work display more similarities than differences. Moreover, recent changes in post-16 funding bind previously disparate services together under the same regulations. The issues raised in this book are, therefore, common to a large number of teachers who can be distinguished by one or more of the following features. They:

■ work with learners who are 19 years of age and older;
■ are predominantly employed on a part-time (often casual) basis;
■ may have few or no teaching qualifications;
■ have limited access to continuing professional development;
■ work with learners who have a wide range of motivations for learning: business or leisure, self improvement or pleasure;
■ may be delivering accredited or non-accredited courses;
■ have a history of competently dealing with change;
■ frequently work in isolated situations with little or no formal supervision and often limited resources;
■ may have limited training in the delivery of their home language as a foreign language;
■ may have little experience and/or knowledge of UK education systems.

There are messages, too, for those in senior management to whom languages programme teachers are responsible. The management structures of adult education do not always allow for curriculum specialists to be in charge. Every specialism will stake its claim to being 'different' with some justification. Managers must recognise and respond to the particular features of their areas of responsibility if there is to be real progress in the quality of teaching.

As well as a manual for teachers, this book seeks to be a 'window on the world' of adult language teaching and learning for all those with an interest in the matter.

Content

In order to become effective practitioners, adult language teachers need to have an understanding of their client group, a broad overview of political and other influences on their work, and be able to function competently in the classroom, making use of a variety of teaching methods and resources. We open the debate on these key features in this book. Suggestions are made throughout about ways in which tutors may pursue theory and practice in their own time.

While the emphasis falls very much on the business of delivering sound language teaching, it is also important to include the theoretical and contextual detail that encompasses this delivery.

Adult education is fast acquiring a new shape for a new century. The notion of lifelong learning lies at the heart of the political agenda that seeks to improve the economic fortunes of the UK and to promote social inclusion. In this context the sector will be scrutinised for its ability to deliver. What is valued is the potential of adult education to support the strong commitment to learning and to contribute to the aims for the future.

It is inevitable that eventually the effects of all this activity will impact on those who actually do the work. There will be changing demands from managers and different learners with different needs and motivations. Our customers are already beginning to display all the signs of the sophisticated consumers that they have become. Used to shopping around and moving on if the right deal does not materialise, potential learners have a very clear idea of the product that they seek. Perhaps this goes some of the way to explaining the alarming statistic highlighted in NIACE's survey (*Tongue tied but trying?*, 1999) that 44% of adults would like to learn a language but only 5% were doing so at the time.

At the time of writing one mode of delivery for language learning predominates, that is the weekly group meeting over a period of up to 30 weeks. While continuing to satisfy the needs of some learners, this model accords ill with the changing lifestyles and expectations of many 21st century participants. New modes of delivery, such as examples of blended learning, family learning, residential, distance and self-access learning, are being tried out across the UK. There is, however, little sign as yet that programme planners are taking account of the fact that, in order to capture the potential audience for language training, a variety of delivery modes is at least as important as variety in the content and range of learning programmes. The accepted model of long slow progress to fluency is not one that is likely to be of appeal to present-day adult learners, particularly those whose home language is global.

We are working in a prevailing climate of 'professionalisation'. Teachers are called on not only to maintain that elusive 'feel good' factor that has always been the hallmark of successful adult work but, at the same time, to approach the task with rigour, to conform to expectations of quality. They need, therefore, to respond to the challenges themselves and, in doing so, will sustain that individuality that has permeated adult courses for decades and that has contributed to the quiet but overwhelming success of teaching languages.

The levels of independence that adult services enjoy remain the envy of many in other education sectors. It is, of course, critical that those who work with adult learners embrace flexible working practices that can be made to conform to the needs and expectations of the learners they seek to serve. For teachers, however, the levels of responsibility that arise from being in sole charge of syllabus, method, resources and outcomes can be daunting. As yet the teaching of languages in adult education has no received methodology or pedagogy. There are a number of frameworks of learner achievement but no consensus about which to apply. Teachers are required to conform to the criteria of the Adult Learning Inspectorate and other quality controls, but these are generic descriptors of best practice in adult education and do not reveal how language teaching should be delivered.

It is precisely this ability to make critical choices about content and method that lies at the heart of the job satisfaction element in adult education and also contributes to its success. This book lays before the reader a range of options of ways to learn, of frameworks, of quality criteria. We raise new approaches and methods. Some respond to the current trend of needing to prove 'value for money'. What are the outcomes of a language-learning experience? How are these best demonstrated? In what ways do they benefit the learner? Others are destined to give a new look to the business of language teaching. To what extent can individual learning be accommodated in group work? What is the place of information technology in language teaching and learning? Traditionalists and those who hold with the notion of 'not throwing the baby out with the bathwater' will be pleased to note that we have also retained some well loved traditional features of language teaching and learning albeit revisited and given a 21st century 'spin'.

But in all of this and in the spirit of the very best of adult education, we leave decisions about what to do and how to do it up to teacher and learners.

How to use the book

The book is part manual, part narrative and essentially outlines the pedagogic shift towards placing the learner at the heart of the process. This key theme is signposted throughout. We encourage teachers, potential and active, to recognise and understand that their job is more about facilitating learning than about delivering teaching.

The complex world of adult education and of teaching languages within it cannot be fully explained nor every response formulated. This book may be viewed as a starting point for the development of ideas and practice. Change, challenge, controversy and triumph in adversity are all features of languages for adults. This work is both celebration and demonstration of best practice and a call to arms for future generations of teachers.

Adults learning languages – the challenge

■ Linda Parker

In this chapter I'd like to go back to some basics, looking first at how adults learn in general, then at what their needs as language learners might be, and finally how all this might apply to how they learn – and how we teach – languages. I'll conclude by drawing up a checklist of some of the things that perhaps we need to consider when planning the languages curriculum for adult learners.

The adult language learner

We all know the typical scenario faced by prospective language learners who attend classes in adult education. They sign up for a class for a fixed period of time, are put into what's usually the ultimate in mixed-ability groups taught by a single tutor, they often follow at least the outline structure of a standard course book, which prescribes what they learn, and, for many, funding arrangements require that they are obliged to take some form of formal assessment.

But is this traditional classroom-based, tutor-centred approach the best way of helping adults to learn languages? Is what's currently on the language-learning menu the best we can offer and might there be other ways of delivering languages in our institutions? Should we reassess our aims for many of our adult learners, taking more account of their own objectives? Are the techniques and strategies we use the most effective ones for this age group? And are there any guidelines on good practice for teachers of languages to adults?

In the past there was a commonly held stereotype, among both learners and teachers, that it was difficult for adults, and especially older adults, to be effective language learners. It was generally accepted that the best time to learn languages was in childhood. A great deal of research has been carried out in this area. Results tend to imply that, provided conditions are right, adults have the potential to learn languages well and that they may even be better than children at certain aspects of language learning (for example understanding semantic relations and developing grammatical sensibility). Attitudes then have changed for the better.

We now know that adults can be good foreign language learners, and more so when their particular aptitudes and needs are taken into account.

In order to consider how we can help adults learn languages more effectively, let's begin by stepping back from the discipline itself and take a look at the characteristics, learning preferences and motivation of adult learners generally. They seem to have certain features in common.

Adult learners:

- are independent and self-directed;
- are goal-orientated;
- like to know that what they're learning is relevant and has purpose;
- are practical and like problem-solving;
- have developed learning strategies in other contexts;
- have accumulated life experiences upon which they can draw.

Research has shown that many adult learners prefer certain kinds of learning.

They like:

- practical and problem-solving approaches;
- working together;
- materials which are relevant and incorporate real-life experiences.

They are not so keen on:

- activities which involve short-term memory;
- learning by rote;
- oral repetition.

Adults are motivated by many things and a more in-depth analysis of the complex motivating factors which lead adults to language learning is discussed in Chapter 2.

In brief, they may come to classes for:

- making social relationships;
- escape;
- stimulation;
- professional development/enhancement;
- immediate practical, personal needs (e.g. holidays);
- interest in the subject.

We must remember that adults have many other responsibilities in their lives (family, work) and that they will certainly have many constraints on their time.

In any group of adult learners, the reasons for learning a language will be diverse – travel, tourism, business, family, owning property abroad, helping children with homework or simply relishing the intellectual challenge.

Learners have their own goals and time frames. Some will want to achieve a fairly low level of proficiency in a relatively short time (the tourist to Greece, for example); others will be hoping to reach a high level of fluency and will see their learning stretching over an extended period (the learner planning to move abroad and who wants to integrate in the local community).

There is very little here that is new or surprising, but it has a direct bearing on the types of language-learning experiences we offer adult learners, the techniques we use and the support we give them, both in and out of the classroom.

We also need to think about what adults bring with them into the language-learning experience which will have a bearing on our planning. Adults embarking on learning a new language will all have preconceived ideas about learning in general and in addition may have:

- preconceived ideas about language learning;
- previous experience of language learning;
- lack of confidence.

We know that potentially some or all of these can have a profound effect on adult language learners, either because they shape their attitudes or because they hinder progress. The student who has had a bad language-learning experience in school comes with a number of hang-ups about what it means to learn a language and lacks confidence in his or her own aptitude as a language learner. Some will think that it's more difficult to learn a language in adult life. Others, often those who were reasonably successful learners in the past, will have fixed ideas about appropriate methodologies and believe that there is only one 'correct' way to learn a language

Adults will certainly have their own learning styles (see more on this below) and will have developed learning strategies which they will have used successfully in the past in other situations.

So what conclusions can be drawn from what's been said so far? What might the impact of all this be on:

- the aims to which we aspire and how these affect the curriculum?
- the methodology and approaches we use?
- the support structures we put in place to ensure that students feel confident, make progress, can discuss problems, ask questions, and don't drop out of classes after the first missed lesson?

We need to bear the adult language learners' goals, expectations and experience in mind when planning our menu for them.

Let's look first at our **aims** and how these relate to the **language–learning opportunities** that we offer in the curriculum.

The traditional pattern of the long, thin course (common in formal education), spread over a number of years with a long-term aim of producing (in the best of all possible worlds) a linguist with a high degree of fluency in the target language (the 'near native speaker' model) is simply not viable when teaching the majority of adults. The goals of many of our students are likely to be quite different and one of the characteristics of adult learners is that they are **goal-orientated**. Their goals may simply be to survive as a tourist or to attempt to speak some of a foreign language as a courtesy to a business or social contact. Others may have very specific needs regarding the purchase of property abroad or being able to chat to the locals in a village where they own a house.

The traditional pattern of the long, thin course is simply not viable when teaching the majority of adults.

In order to cope with the diversity of learning goals we might consider:

- more short, sharp courses;
- more materials designed for the needs of certain groups;
- providing the learner with 'jumping-off' points beyond which they can pursue their language-learning on their own but with advice and support where necessary;
- flexibility to move in and out of formal classes;
- drop-in sessions;
- workshops on various aspects of language learning which could be generic (e.g. *How to learn vocabulary* or *Improving your listening skills*) or language/culture specific (e.g. *Reading a Spanish contract*);
- blended learning approaches which incorporate a mixture of setting, and a considerable degree of ICT support (i.e. on-line BBC materials specifically designed for adults, commercially available software, etc).

Opportunities like these might also help provide support for those hundreds of thousands of language learners who never get as far as a class but who teach themselves using off-the-shelf materials, TV and Internet courses, etc. Workshops, support sessions and similar activities may bring new learners through the doors.

Some of these things are already happening in some places. They may require more flexible thinking than some senior managers are used to and do not necessarily fit into current funding structures, but they could be a way forward and help to provide the diversity of opportunity that may be needed to create the conditions for more successful learning.

The Language Centre at Nottingham Trent University teaches around 2,000 non-specialist students a year in a range of European and Oriental languages. Students attending courses come from both the university student population, university staff and also – about 20% a year – from the wider community. Most courses last 24 weeks and are fairly traditional in the sense that they are led by specialist tutors (many of them native speakers) and normally follow standard course books. However, alongside the taught programme runs a parallel 'Independent Learning' programme – tailor-made for each group – which suggests activities and extension work to help students to internalise, memorise and go beyond what has been taught in class. Students also have access to an open learning centre, with its own dedicated language advisers, whose job is to support student language learning. They provide generic support materials (e.g. Improving your listening skills; How to learn vocabulary), run workshops and give one-to-one advice sessions. The advisers are not there to provide expertise on individual languages, but to complement the language tutor by adding another dimension to the learning experience.

A UK led Lingua 1 project – **the ALLEGRO project** – is exploring the use of study circles for language learning as a way of supporting learners in rural communities or those studying less widely-learnt and taught languages. Partners in the UK and Slovenia have set up study circles where students are working independently at learning languages; each group has a support worker who may be a languages teacher but is not an expert in the language concerned.

In 2002 **Leicester Adult Education College** offered drop-in sessions and extra activities for a group of students learning German. Here the tutor, Annett Hering, who is also Co-ordinator of Languages in the College, describes how they worked:

'The drop-in sessions were not officially advertised but I offered them to my Level 1 German students twice. I suppose I am privileged because I am full time and can do little extras like that... The sessions ran over one-and-a-half hours and students could come and go as they wished. Both sessions were attended by a small group of approximately eight people and the idea was to introduce them to the BBC website, which most of the students had not seen/used before. This was successful in so far as students worked with the *Talk German* book, cassettes and video clips during class time and at home and the website offered them a different approach and resource which they enjoyed. Some of the students had not often used a computer and after the introduction they really got into it. For me it was a chance to test the materials, which I really like. I had to do this outside class time as we were not usually in the room with the computers.

For the second session I had invited another native speaker and students could test their communicative skills with her.

The German Day was another extra event in addition to traditional classes, and among other things we worked with tourist information websites from Jena and Cologne that day. Students were asked to plan a day out in these cities.

We are hoping to take a group of learners to Weimar next year – so, if you like, these are all added activities to promote a language that's a little deprived at the moment...'

When it comes to making choices about **methodology**, we need to take a close look again at those characteristics of adult learners.

Learner independence

This is a hard one for language teachers and learners, especially when teaching complete beginners. More than in many other subjects, the learner of a new language starts out as almost entirely dependent on the teacher. But it is in all our interests to move learners from this dependent role, through a collaborative phase, to being an independent language learner. The skills and strategies learnt along the way may ultimately be of more value to them as a **lifelong language learner** than the level of competence acquired in the individual language concerned.

> *We need to focus much more in our classes on the development of language-learning strategies, on empowering learners and letting them go.*

Taking this step is just as difficult for the learner as it is for the teacher. Teachers are used to being in control, learners are often happy to allow them to be. Taking responsibility for your own learning can be a frightening experience. So the steps must be carefully planned. Independence doesn't mean that you don't need support and advice, but that you are fully engaged in your own learning, can make your own decisions and develop your own learning strategies.

Much has been written in this area in recent years and tutors will find no difficulty in identifying useful guidance materials. A good start for those interested in reading more about independence and learner autonomy is *The good practice guide* on the website of the Subject Centre for Languages, Linguistics and Area Studies (see Appendix, p131).

➤ ➤ Adults are **practical and like problem-solving**

The use of problem-solving activities is an interesting and exciting one for both language teachers and language learners. It is certainly not a new concept in language teaching and provides a wealth of opportunities in the languages classroom. It can be used from the earliest stages of language teaching, for example in the simple and familiar pair-work and group information-gap exercises commonly used to practise the language of personal identity. With 'intermediate' learners more exciting opportunities occur.

I have regularly used a tried and trusted exercise with groups of all ages and abilities which was originally based on the Baker Street Game in Friederike Klippel's *Keep talking – communicative fluency activities for language teaching* (pp112–113). The game involves a whole class in a puzzle/problem-solving activity in which previously learned language can be used in an authentic and interesting way, which requires class co-operation and involves all students in both reading and speaking. Although the game, as described in the book, relates to the language of personal identity, it can be adapted to many different topics and situations. This exercise takes time to prepare and requires plenty of time in the classroom, but it is an excellent example of how time well spent in preparation can pay dividends in teaching.

With advanced classes all kinds of complex problem-solving activities can be devised. These often work well in combination with role-playing exercises and again can lead to lengthy classroom activities. An example of this kind of approach might be a role play based on a proposed commercial development in a rural area where students take on the roles of local inhabitants, developers, planners and must ultimately reach agreement on a local development plan. The only limit to the scope of advanced problem solving activities is probably the teacher's own imagination. However, given the demands on teachers in terms of preparation, it is reassuring to know that activities like these work well with adult learners. More examples for both new and more advanced learners are given in Chapter 4 in particular.

> ➤ ➤ Adults have accumulated **life experiences** upon which they can draw

Many languages classrooms are very teacher-centred, but providing opportunities for adult learners to work together, sharing problems and experiences may help to build learners' confidence. This may mean creating opportunities for learners to discuss problems which have arisen in reinforcement work outside the classroom and is in itself an excellent reason for ensuring that learners have a programme of 'homework' or 'independent learning' to follow. Allowing for time like this to be set aside in an already crammed course may seem to some to be a loss of valuable teaching time and to introduce even more English into what many believe should be essentially a target language environment. Nevertheless, I would argue that finding time for discussion of this kind will help many learners take the step towards taking responsibility for their own learning and also help to create a supportive and open atmosphere.

Another way of integrating learners' life experiences is in creating activities to which learners are able to bring experience from outside the immediate language-learning context. The role-playing activity described above would be a good example of this for advanced learners and it is equally possible to come up with similar ideas for the less advanced student.

Where **previous experience of language learning** has not been good, group activities, especially when it comes to things like learning vocabulary, oral practice and repetition (highlighted above as being less popular with adult learners), which take away the fear of individual embarrassment, may be a good classroom technique.

> ➤ ➤ Adults like to know that what they're learning is **relevant** and has purpose

We need to ensure that new ideas and new language is presented in contexts which the learner recognises as true to life and relevant. Language teaching is fortunate in this respect, we constantly refer to the real world and real-life situations. But adults need to know why they are learning things and that what they are learning is applicable and transferable. They need to feel in control of what they're learning. For example, they may know lots of vocabulary or have memorised the right phrases to deal with a number of transactional situations, but often they cannot generate language for themselves and have no idea of how the language fits together. We need to give our students the basic building blocks of the language.

The emphasis on the four skills has been a feature of language teaching at all levels in recent years. But how often do we explicitly teach students **how** to listen, for example? Yet without guidance on this many students may feel uncomfortable, lost and not understand the relevance of the task.

We need to provide a very mixed diet in our classes and include language awareness, grammar, developing specific language skills.

Learning styles

> ➤ ➤ Adults **have their own individual learner style and have developed learning strategies in other contexts**

Much work has been done in recent years on learning styles. Basically this means that as learners we do not all think and learn in the same way. Some of us will be at our most receptive when presented with information in written form, others might prefer visual stimuli, while some will respond more to the presentation of new ideas through physical activity or music. We are influenced by our particular learning styles in all that we attempt to learn and when students learn a new language, they will adopt general approaches based on their own learning style. The References at the end of this chapter recommend some introductory reading if you'd like to find out more about learning styles and there is also a discussion in Chapter 2.

Vark – a guide to learning styles (see Appendix, p131) – is an interesting website where you can do an on-line questionnaire to assess your own learning style. It also gives an insight into the kinds of strategies that might appeal to different learning styles. For example, a learner who responds to visual stimuli will learn better from a teacher who uses gestures, textbooks with lots of diagrams or pictures, videos, posters, use of colour in presentation, or symbols; a 'kinesthetic' (a 'doing') learner will be helped by hands-on approaches, methods which employ the senses, abstract principles made concrete by examples. Some learners will favour step-by-step learning, others will respond to a more global approach. Faced with all this, where do we start? How do we begin to structure a language-learning menu which could cater for even this fairly short round-up of learning styles? A recent slogan claimed: *'The more ways you teach, the more people you reach'*. I suspect that there's a message here for language teachers about the importance of variety.

In addition to being aware of learners and their individual learning styles, it is also essential to develop an awareness of one's own preferences as a teacher. It might just be that because a teacher is an auditory type, he or she overuses this particular style.

> *Our own learning style will have an influence on how we teach languages to our students.*

It isn't just teachers who need to be aware of learning styles, it is also likely to be an unfamiliar concept to the learners themselves and will need to be made explicit by working with students to help them to recognise that there is more than one way of learning, and exploring with them various strategies and techniques. Take for example learning vocabulary. How do you learn new words? Perhaps you:

- categorise – by initial letter, by topic, etc;
- keep a vocabulary book;
- keep writing them down;
- put post-its on the fridge;
- learn by heart;
- learn a certain number a day;
- learn with another person and like to be tested;
- look for patterns;
- look for links between words;
- link words and mental pictures;
- learn words in context.

> *We need to help students to develop language-learning strategies which are appropriate for them as individuals.*

Suggesting different ways in which students may learn new words, pointing out that different ways suit different people and giving examples will help learners to understand the concept of learning styles and to find ways of learning that suit them best. The book *DIY techniques for language learners* by María Fernández–Toro and Francis R Jones offers a series of questionnaires to help learners decide what learning approaches suit them best, and then provides a range of learning techniques for developing the various skills.

We need to incorporate into our menu language-learning opportunities, methods of instruction and learning activities which appeal to different types of learners. Supporting our learners' invividual needs through a variety of teaching approaches isn't necessarily new and it isn't rocket science; it's part and parcel of what good teachers have always done.

Teacher development

So far we've focused on adult learners and what they bring with them to the language-learning situation, but it's probably also worth considering at this point what language teachers bring with them to the classroom. If we are to reconsider some of the ways we think about teaching languages to adults, then we will almost certainly need to change the attitudes of some teachers.

The first and perhaps the most important thing that language teachers bring to the classroom is how we were taught or learnt ourselves. The following is from an essay by an American linguist, Linda Chance:

> 'The process of learning a language is such a challenge to the ego, I believe, that we all carry scars and attachments to the irrational parts of our linguistic identities and the methods that saved us.'

It is very hard to escape from these 'scars and attachments', however hard we try. A lifetime later, I still find myself teaching students to use techniques that were successful for me as a secondary school pupil. And among consenting adults I personally am a 'learn the grammar and do the exercises' addict, because that's what worked for me as a child; as a learner myself I need to read, write and translate to begin to get to grips with a new language. However, there is a danger that these may be the only methods we pass on to our own students and we cannot rely on them being effective for everyone.

Nowadays, with the far greater range of languages being taught in post-19 education and greater teacher mobility, tutors are more likely to be native speakers, especially if the language concerned is an unusual one. These teachers bring with them a wonderful resource as they have the rich cultural background of the native speaker upon which to draw. They are able to add a cultural and intercultural dimension to their teaching which the non-native teacher can only dream of. The best native teachers integrate these elements into their teaching: the Spanish teacher who uses her passion for flamenco to inspire her learners; the German teacher, originally trained as an artist, who takes her students around local art galleries, encouraging them to use their German to discuss the German works of art; the teacher of primary French who is able to reach back into his own childhood as he teaches nursery rhymes and simple stories to his groups.

Native speaking teachers also bring the culture of language teaching used in their own countries and this can have both advantages and drawbacks.

One real advantage can be when teachers use resources, course books or other stimuli, which are produced in the country of the target language. These reflect the culture of that country more realistically than resources produced elsewhere and are perhaps less likely to lead to cultural stereotyping. Those non-native teachers among us, educated and trained in the UK, rely too heavily perhaps on teaching resources produced in this country. On the other hand, when the cultural dimension extends to methodology, problems can arise. Teachers from countries where there is a single predominant teaching method, and who transfer this to their teaching in adult classes in this country, may not be successful in the mixed-ability, mixed-background environment that is the typical UK adult classroom.

All this points us towards training. The days of completely unqualified staff teaching languages to adults seem to be numbered, but there are still many staff with low-level qualifications and restricted access to in-service training. They may have little or no opportunity to observe other staff at work and few chances to get together with their peers to discuss issues of common concern. Those lucky enough to work in institutions where support for tutors is good, where there is funding and time allowed for in-service training, where senior management has a clear commitment to the professional development of part-time or casually employed staff will know how lucky they are. There are signs, however, that the hitherto impoverished support for tutors of adults is set to improve. Government quality targets, inspection, new UK policies on languages education, the growth of the specialist schools (in our case Language Colleges) may all contribute to the steady improvement in training opportunities. However, we still need to look for innovative and cost-effective ways of delivering staff training; even more crucial is to find ways of convincing staff of the importance of training.

> *Professional development is vital to teachers as individuals, it is the key to their success as teachers and to their own progress through the profession.*

One size doesn't fit all

I promised at the beginning of this chapter that I would conclude by making some suggestions about what the future of languages in adult education might look like and offering a checklist of things we might consider for the more effective delivery of languages in this sector.

One of the things that seems clear to me is that the common factors which appear to influence many adult learners, and the constraints under which the majority operates, suggest that a more learner-centred approach from teachers might be effective. We can no longer simply offer linear 'one size fits all' courses. **We must find out more about why our students want to learn, perhaps through questionnaires or short interviews, and we must attempt to offer opportunities for language learning which fit those needs.**

If our students are to make steady progress, working in ways which suit them as individuals and engaging with and taking control of their own language learning – which they must do to become a successful language learner – then much of that work has to be done outside the classroom. **The challenge for us as teachers is how to motivate learners to engage in this way, how to monitor and support them and how to cope with students progressing at different rates.**

The aim of the National Strategy for Languages, *Languages for all: languages for life*, is to improve our national capability in languages. If we are to do this in an effective way in lifelong learning, then perhaps we need to broaden and rethink the role that adult education plays. As well as offering traditional language classes, for which there will always be a place, future provision could include more flexible learning opportunities.

The potential of ICT

An area that I've avoided so far is that of Information and Communication Technology (ICT) and Information and Learning

Technology (ILT) (see Appendix, p130, for an indication of the difference between these terms), but so crucial is it to future development that I can't avoid it any longer. We all know the problems that ICT/ILT poses in adult education: the lack of basic equipment in many institutions, no money for software, the huge variance in the appropriate skills of language teachers, the lack of money to provide them with basic training. But it is a changing picture and there is improvement in all these areas. A very short time ago, if you asked most language teachers in adult education if they used the Internet and e-mail, the answer was a resounding no. Today, if you ask the same question, the response is likely to be much more positive. Teachers are beginning to have more experience of using ICT/ILT at home, and although the thought of using it in the classroom may still be a daunting – or through lack of hardware and resources even an impossible – one, attitudes are gradually changing and its potential is increasingly recognised.

> *The potential of communication technology in supporting learners is huge.*

At the simplest level, e-mail communication with students opens up a new channel of support with impressive features. With a couple of clicks of the mouse you can send information to a whole group of students, you can follow up those who have missed classes, send ideas for extension work. Students can e-mail one another, practise using the target language between themselves, circulate their own ideas or information. It's a perfect way to build your class into a virtual language-learning community. It won't suit everyone, of course, but for some students it will be an ideal way to encourage their learning outside the classroom.

The Internet also provides us with a wealth of opportunities to bring the world of languages into our classrooms and to our students. Even if computers or Internet access are not yet to be found in all our institutions, it is already in many teachers' and students' homes and it can be built into our teaching. (See Chapter 4, p90, for some strategies on how to use the Internet in the classroom.) Again, the potential of extending learning beyond the classroom is enormous.

The growth of e-Learning will be another key area. Important pilot projects for languages are already underway with big national and international players developing innovative new ways of teaching languages. How will adult education respond to and interface with these new initiatives, which could bring even more adults – who may still need opportunities for face-to-face practice and support – into language learning? Is this another challenge which might be met through flexible provision?

The emerging picture

The picture of adult education which begins to emerge is an exciting one which offers:

- short and long courses;
- drop-in workshops;
- facilities for students to come for language-learning advice and support;
- open learning centres where students would have access to technology and resources;
- on-line support structures;
- trained staff, familiar with the needs of adult learners;
- information of all kinds on language learning.

Provision of languages education to adults in any one area may be spread over a number of collaborating institutions and services and could include:

- an Adult Education college;
- FE colleges;
- classes in local Community schools and centres;
- local specialist Language Colleges;
- university Language Centres;
- university Continuing Education departments;
- private providers.

There seems to be a strong case for better collaboration between institutions and for structured support to help this happen.

The Regional Development Agencies and the work they are currently doing to support languages could be a catalyst for closer collaboration between institutions, as would financial support to encourage collaborative ventures. For example, some institutions, like universities, have excellent but sometimes under-used independent learning facilities, often specifically for language learning. Perhaps funding could be made available for enhanced staffing and longer opening hours in the university for the benefit of students and staff in less well-equipped establishments. Without some financial incentive it is unlikely that such collaborations will happen as a matter of course.

Similarly, the introduction of an entitlement curriculum at KS4 will inevitably have an impact on available teachers for the adult education sectors. With schools opting out of compulsory language teaching at 14, some teachers may find themselves available to teach in post-19 institutions, bringing with them their experience and pedagogical approaches.

In order to move towards many of the things I've talked about here, we shouldn't need to reinvent the wheel. In universities, for example, much work has been done in the fields of learner autonomy and professional development which would be easily and immediately transferable to adult education. Language tutors in universities have found themselves in the same circumstances as those working in adult education (and indeed increasingly they may in fact be the same peripatetic teachers). In recent years the trend has been away from undergraduate students studying languages as major components of degrees, towards languages in combination with other subjects or in addition to a main subject. This has meant a large increase in the number of learners studying languages as complete or near beginners for two or three hours a week. Many of those teaching these students are not full-time members of academic staff but hourly-paid or part-time language tutors. And many of these are unqualified or partly qualified native speakers. The similarities to the situation in other parts of post-19 education do not need to be spelt out. Higher education has responded to these new demands in a number of ways, and in many institutions there has been a considerable level of investment in both infrastructure (new Language Centres, for example) and the investigation of new pedagogical approaches.

So, there's help out there if you know where to look. The Appendix (p131) provides a short list of free in-service training support materials and courses, and the References (p20) suggest further reading which could lead to new initiatives in some of those areas mentioned here.

Finally, we come to that summative checklist I promised at the very start of this chapter. It's by no means definitive but might help to focus attention or stimulate discussion in your institution and among your colleagues.

checklist

☐ Find out why students are learning a language and design learning opportunities which fit in with those needs.

☐ Introduce more flexibility into languages programmes.

☐ Consider the possibility of running more short courses.

☐ Build learner autonomy and confidence.

☐ Introduce workshops and drop-in sessions.

☐ See our language learners as part of the wider learning community – make explicit the transferable skills they acquire as language learners.

☐ See ourselves as learning strategy trainers as well as language teachers.

☐ Recognise different learner styles and the need to build a variety of activities into our teaching and help students to develop learner strategies appropriate to them. No two learners are alike – find out what works for your learners.

☐ Use approaches and techniques which are appropriate for adult learners and avoid those which they may find threatening.

☐ Give learners the building bricks of a language – the components they need to put a language together – and give them 'ownership', the potential to be creative and the ability to generate new language for themselves.

☐ Provide better support mechanisms, harnessing the potential of new technology where appropriate.

References

Chance, L. (1998) 'Education in Asian languages. *Education about Asia*, Volume 3, Number 3, Winter.

DfES (2002) *Languages for all: languages for life – the National Languages Strategy for England*.

Fernández-Toro, M. and Jones, F. R. (2001) *DIY techniques for language learners*. CILT.

Gardner, H. (1983) *Frames of mind: the theory of multiple intelligences*. New York: Basic

Klippel, F. (1984) *Keep talking – communicative fluency activities for language teaching*. Cambridge University Press.

Krashen, S. D., Long, M. A. and Scarcella, R. C. (1979) 'Age, rate and evaluation. Attainment in second language acquisition'. *TESOL Quarterly* 13: 573–582.

Mc Laughlin, B. (1992) *Myths and misconceptions about second language learning: what every teacher needs to unlearn*. National Center for Research on Cultural Diversity and Second Language Learning Educational Practice Report 5.

Schleppegrell, M. (1987) *The older language learner, ERIC*. Clearing House on Languages and Linguistics, Number 287313.

Participation, expectation and motivation

■ Fran Beaton

Every year large numbers of adult learners join classes in Community, Adult, Further and Higher Education for reasons as diverse as the learners themselves. Their reasons may be any or all of the following: personal, recreational, social, vocational or academic. Who are these learners, and what are their expectations? What motivates them to learn a language – and, crucially, what deters those who say they want to learn, but do not in fact take part in any kind of formal course?

Participation in language learning

From school to university

In the last decade alone, the profile of language learning and teaching in the United Kingdom has undergone major change. The numbers of school students studying even one language to the age of 16 has declined steadily. The restructuring of the AS/A2 curriculum in 2000 does not seem to have changed the picture, and university applications for specialist languages degrees tell a similar story. Mike Kelly, responding to government, calls for a 50% increase in those participating in Higher Education by 2010. He points out that:

> *'Languages are seen as difficult, and are more studied in the independent than the state sector ... and are increasingly being marked as belonging to a social elite.'*

Kelly makes a powerful case for universities addressing this with a range of external partners. The current consensus appears to be that a collaborative approach between education providers, the public and voluntary sectors would help widen the appeal of language study.

Language-learning provision needs to be increasingly accessible to non-specialists. Such provision must address the fundamental needs and aspirations of the traditional adult education constituency as well as to encourage into learning those who feel that it is not for them.

Adult, Community and Further Education services are uniquely positioned to provide all kinds of people with varied opportunities for trying out – or continuing – their learning in different formats, in different ways and in non-traditional locations.

Adult language learning

Statistics from the Learning and Skills Council (LSC), the body responsible for post-16 Adult, Community and Further Education funding, show that over 2.5 million learners joined accredited vocational courses in 2001/2002. The Adult and Community Learning Fund, set up in 1998 specifically to engage *'disadvantaged or marginalised adults ...*

(in) 'first rung' or informal learning delivered in familiar community surroundings' (DfES 2002) estimates that 130,000 adults who had not previously engaged in learning have participated in numerous initiatives since the fund's inception.

However, there remains a largely untapped potential student body. NIACE, in its 2002 survey, interviewed a weighted sample of adults nationwide and reached the following conclusions

- 90% believed learning made a positive difference both at a personal and employment level;
- 42% had engaged in learning in the last three years;
- nearly 75% believed that 'learning is not for the likes of us'.

There was also clear evidence that age, professional status, region, recent involvement in learning and access to IT were powerful factors in determining whether an individual participated in learning or not.

The most comprehensive report on participation in adult language learning (Tuckett & Cara) suggests that 58% of those surveyed spoke only one language. 44% of the monolingual respondents would like to learn a language, even though only 5% are currently doing so. The report also provides evidence that the largest proportion of languages learners come from higher social classes – 65% have professional and management responsibility compared with 28% of unskilled workers. There are also marked regional differences: more people speak additional languages in Greater London and Wales than they do in Scotland or the West Midlands. The report also includes interesting data on participants' gender (men and women speak the same number of languages), age (participation is greater among younger adults) and the range of languages in which people are interested – an impressive total of 60.

The business case

In addition to meeting the aspirations of individuals, it is increasingly important to view languages training as part of the wider political context that identifies the need to improve the skills of the UK workforces in order to underpin and sustain economic prosperity.

The Nuffield Languages Inquiry, the most ambitious and exhaustive single national survey of the state of language learning, highlighted particularly the dangers of monolingualism, especially among English speaking communities.

The United Kingdom is a player in the European and global economies, with significant trading and business links worldwide. This does not, however, mean that our business partners and competitors should or will be prepared to do business in English, simply for the reason that the English colleague is monolingual. Nor is the underlying assumption of monolingualism – a lack of curiosity or interest in another culture, or its language – one which is likely to oil the wheels of commerce. Monolingual professionals are also limited in their career opportunities.

> *'The majority of young people in the UK leave school, college or university with little useful competence in languages and no transnational, cross-cultural work experience. Meanwhile, our European and Asian competitors are producing people who are at least as well qualified technically, and speak good English alongside a range of other languages – enabling them to be posted overseas at short notice.'* (2000:19)

It may be worth pointing to regional language strategies which are being developed collaboratively by regional language networks and Regional Development Agencies (RDAs) in response to this analysis of need, translating national priorities and trends into regional and local solutions.

Which language to learn?

For many learners the question answers itself: there may be family, professional or integrative reasons for pursuing a particular language. However, there have been periods in which specific languages have been prioritised at national level. In the 1960s, for example, Russian enjoyed a brief but lively renaissance.

From a business point of view, the Nuffield findings cite German, Spanish and French as the most important languages, due to the rapid development of trading links both with Europe and Latin America. However, the global marketplace means that trade links – particularly with countries to which the UK wishes to export – must be robustly established and maintained with the new rich nations: China, Japan and the Arab world. Proficiency in languages such as Portuguese and Russian also extends business and trading opportunities. As linguists we may take the view that the fact of learning another language is enough in itself, and that it is less relevant which one. However, if education providers are to make their mark in the commercial world and persuade those who do not speak a language that it is a worthwhile activity, then the commercial benefits of language learning need to be clear.

> *Education providers need to promote the commercial benefits of language learning, especially in the context of regional requirements and potential.*

This in turn means focusing on how to embed and describe learning in ways which are clear and relevant to learners and employers; reflecting on how we teach; and on where and how we teach it. Let us also not forget the 60 languages which respondents of that NIACE survey said they would like to learn if they had the chance.

Expectations

The ways in which post-16 courses are devised, funded and delivered have changed almost beyond recognition in the last decade. It is worth stressing here that while these changes have had a major effect on curriculum and practice, the reasons for which learners continue to learn have remained remarkably stable.

Commercial language-learning advertisements suggest that learning a language is deceptively easy, whereas languages teachers tend to be of the opinion that it takes years to achieve a high level of competence.

> *If the gap between what learners expect and what they get appears too great, learners will get discouraged.*

In the first stages of learning a language the sense of achievement is usually very high, there then comes a stage when learners feel that their meteoric progress has slowed down. More advanced students may be so focused on what they are **not** yet able to use the language for, that they discount the progress they have already made.

A shared sense of purpose and achievement is crucial to maintaining motivation. It is the tutor's role to help learners to an understanding of what are reasonable expectations of a language-learning experience; to indicate how outcomes will be achieved and to demonstrate that the journey has been successfully undertaken.

The language-learning experience

Most learners have preferred approaches to learning (Rogers 1992: 14–15):

■ **concrete experience**: learning directly by being involved;
■ **reflexive observation**: watching before deciding to act;
■ **abstract conceptualisation**: applying what has been learnt from one experience to another;
■ **active experimentation**: devising and trying out new approaches to see what happens.

Students' attitudes are further modified by the extent to which individuals are used to identifying their own wishes and needs and planning how to achieve them. However, it should not be assumed – even for the more self-aware learners – that they will necessarily be able to identify the steps which will lead to the fulfilment of an ambition to, say, speak French.

Adult learners bring to the classroom experience a combination of any or all of the following:

➤ ➤ their own self- image as a member of society

Most adults have a number of multiple roles and experiences upon which to draw, e.g. they may be any or all of the following: carer, parent, employee, employer.

In addition they may pursue a range of leisure or voluntary activities in the community. The role of 'learner' draws on an individual's perception of how 'being a learner' fits in with these other roles and commitments.

➤ ➤ an individual's self-image as a learner

Adults' perception of themselves as learners is usually based on previous experiences, both within and outside the traditional classroom setting. This perception includes concepts of what it means to be an effective learner, success measured in informal or formal terms (e.g. the ability to communicate, performance in exams), ideas about how the individual learns (learning styles and strategies). These may be the result of self-awareness/scrutiny, based on generational attitudes, or previous experience, whether successful or not.

➤ ➤ an idea of how learning is achieved

This includes questions as to teacher-learner interaction, i.e. the respective roles and responsibilities of the teacher and the learner, and concepts of how learning takes place. Attitudes about what it means to be a learner and what to expect from a teacher are usually grounded in previous experiences or pedagogic traditions.

Some learners may expect the tutor to be **the only reliable source** of all knowledge. They may minimise or avoid contact with fellow learners on the grounds that they can only be 'wrong'. Still others may be so insecure that they are constantly checking new learning against other sources. 'My other/last tutor said …'

Others may be more **group-focused**, defining their own sense of progress by means of the group's sense of progress overall. Rogers (1999: 31) refers to '… *legends about whole groups of friends and neighbours who shop around for a class, any class, that will take them all*.' In my own institution a language class bonded to the extent that in years when there were not enough students to keep the class viable, the students decamped *en bloc* with the tutor to meet in each other's homes before optimistically reappearing the following year. Other learners may be equally keen, but motivated more by **individual goals** than by the sense of group identity.

In all these instances, the combination of different perceptions of who is responsible for what and how the individuals see themselves in relation to others is important in terms of how a group of learners behaves.

Learning in groups

The dynamics within a classroom, or other traditional learning environment, may affect how learners perceive themselves in relation to others, both initially and over a period of time. In other words, the generalised role of 'learner' is refined by the composition of the group.

Individuals may see themselves as being, for example,

- someone who looks after others;
- the reliable one;
- the odd one out;
- the most effective learner in a group;
- the least effective learner in a group.

This perception is honed over time to provide a sense of identity. Clearly, where these perceptions are negative, or trap an individual in a role he or she may have assumed as a temporary camouflage, it is possible for a learner to feel isolated, thus increasing the likelihood of dropping out. An individual's self-image may or may not be accurate, but it is a powerful means of identifying status within any given group, and the traditional classroom, with its closed face-to face dynamics, may serve to underpin that.

These attitudes affect, or are affected by, the dynamics within a group. Thus, the individual who seeks an excessive amount of the teacher's attention in a group of learners may be regarded as unsettling an otherwise stable group dynamic. A learner who does not acknowledge other learners' contributions as viable, and has eyes and ears only for the teacher, may become frustrated if the classroom style is determinedly democratic and centred on the contribution each learner has to make. Fellow students are also likely to become impatient with someone who appears not to acknowledge or value them. However, the teacher can introduce activities which encourage groups to act together in order to accomplish a task (see Chapter 1, p13 – the Baker Street game; also Chapter 4, p56 – the murder mystery; and p63 – jigsaw reading).

Motivation

The nature of language learning

We use language to communicate with others in order to elicit and give information, to express wishes, desires, needs and ambitions, to seek and present opinions. Different registers and the cultural conventions which govern these registers – the context, the medium, the people involved – are complex and may not exist in the learner's mother tongue. We use language as a means of identifying ourselves with a group, or of putting a distance between us and others. When we embark on learning a foreign language, we accept the possibility of change. Potential changes may be of cultural perspective, changes in the way in which beliefs and ideas are communicated, and changes in the way in which one views the world – both the known and the new.

For the learner of languages, looking at different ways of doing things or expressing ideas may involve re-evaluating what has until then been regarded as a given, a fixed point. Some learners will expect and welcome this process, while others regard it as a threat to an individual's or a group's sense of identity. This may engender comments such as 'Why do they do it/say it that way? Why don't they do it like us?'

For many language learners, however, the challenge of the new is seen as part of the interest and excitement of learning a new language and can be a powerful force.

It is important for teachers to ensure that the classroom experience conveys this exciting dimension of language learning in order to motivate learners to be prepared for the hard work and the investment of time and money which is needed.

> *Setting out to learn a foreign language involves the possibility of change.*

Motivation may be:

- **instrumental** – i.e. short-term and goal oriented, suggesting a discrete and finite approach, e.g. such as required by a learner who simply needs basic transactional Greek for a holiday or business trip; or
- **integrative** – i.e. a more generally applied, infinite and deeper interest in learning generally, e.g. if a learner wants to become fluent so he or she can be accepted in a foreign community.

> *Learning a language is extremely rewarding, providing a window on other cultures and enabling us to become active, responsive and thoughtful players on the global stage.*

The difference between the two types of motivation can be seen, in languages, in areas such as pronunciation and grammatical accuracy, where the 'instrumental' learner will not worry too much as long as the message gets across, while the 'integrative' learner will try to perfect accent, intonation and grammatical precision.

It has to be said, though, that the processes involved are frequently more complex than these distinctions suggest. Jenny Rogers (ibid: 33) cites the following example:

> '... about half-way through my Open University degree I realised that I had proved I could do it, and didn't really 'need' to go on. By then I was thoroughly hooked; I couldn't give it up. I just loved the feeling that I was plugging into the best academic knowledge in such a wide range of subjects. As soon as I got the degree, I enrolled for something else.'

> *The learners' motivation will be affected by their perception that they have achieved – or are in the process of achieving – a specific goal or not.*

Whether instrumental or integrative, motivation will remain high if an individual's attempts are met with a warm and positive response. The quality of the response is likely to prompt learners to re-evaluate, consciously or unconsciously, their or the teacher's effectiveness, with either positive or negative consequences. Some learners, faced with a cool reaction, may be spurred to greater effort. Others may decide that they, or the teacher, are not equal to the task and become frustrated, resentful, potential dropouts. Still others may conclude that their original goal was over-ambitious, and aim for something which seems more attainable.

An English mother-tongue speaker had passed two languages at A level, and is currently studying one of these in an advanced class. She is also learning Spanish and Modern Greek ab initio. Her goal is 'to be as articulate in any foreign language as I am in English'. The enthusiasm of the tutor, an increasing sense of confidence in her ability to use the language as she wishes and 'a huge irritation with the British desire to remain monolingual' are key motivating factors.

A Dutch mother-tongue speaker studied German at school and as an element at university. She is chiefly interested in refining her use of the language, as she uses it increasingly at work, but also cites 'a general interest in maintaining linguistic skills'.

Her motivation is chiefly maintained through a sense of being challenged, her ability to use the language in the work environment and the sense of being in a group with a common purpose, and an enthusiastic tutor. Ironically, the increasing demands at work have made it harder for her to attend classes and maintain her high motivation.

A sense of progress, and the teacher's positive and enthusiastic attitude to teaching, are key elements in keeping learners motivated.

For readers who prefer visual representations, a diagram of this process appears below (Jarvis 1995 1: 25).

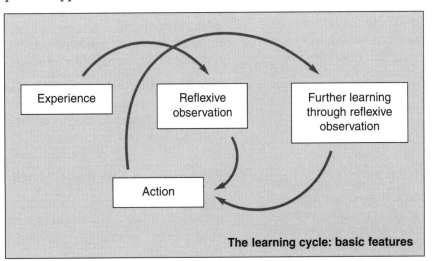

The learning cycle: basic features

One of the differences between **goal oriented** and **deep** (internalised) learning is that the latter involves a plateau period which may appear to the learner to be a stage when little or no learning is taking place, with consequent negative effects on motivation. In fact, during this period a number of skills are being refined. Information is being transferred from the short-term to the working memory. Ways in which this information can be manipulated are explored before that knowledge is either internalised or rejected. For example, language learners encountering a new tense for the first time will initially consider how useful it seems to be, then practise it with vocabulary they already know in a situation where it appears relevant. If that produces positive results, learners will then be encouraged to experiment with other possible combinations, to speed up their delivery and thereby increase their confidence.

A learner's ability to **retrieve information** quickly, or in conjunction with other previously separate items, is a vital skill. It is for the tutor to anticipate the plateau stage and ensure that learners are offered sufficiently challenging and varied tasks to deal positively with this deeper level of learning.

> *High-quality information and advice are not just essential for the learning experience of individuals but also go a long way towards reducing drop-out rates of learners who find themselves in inappropriate courses.*

Laying the foundation

If we accept that language is about communication, then the least we can do for actual and prospective learners is to spell out as clearly as possible what the learner will be able to do.

How much advice is available? Is it clear to potential learners how to access it? The advice may be about the curriculum in general, subject-specific advice, or advice about financial or other support services which the institution can offer (see case study opposite).

Once the learner has joined a particular group, the teacher and the other students are likely to be the base (that sense of belonging again!), but at the early stage of considering returning to learning, the prospective learner will be viewing the institution holistically.

It is not possible for most of us to take radical steps to change the actual physical environment in which we work, but there is a lot that we can do to make the human welcome as warm as possible.

Similarly, the ways in which the curriculum is designed and presented will affect how attractive – or not – it appears to prospective learners. How clear is the information provided? Is it accessible and attractive? Does the emphasis appear to be on the enjoyment of learning, achieving particular personal goals, assessment or a combination of all these? Is the course delivery inclusive? Does the timing or method of delivery exclude particular groups?

One example of this would be a daytime course, aimed at attracting women returners to study, and held at times compatible with school hours and/or with crèche provision (see Chapter 1, p18, for further suggestions).

> *The more focused, informative and helpful the experience of the learning environment is, the more likely it is that an individual's motivation will be high.*

Keeping up the good work

Let us look now at what considerations apply to strategies for maintaining motivation once individual learners have joined a course. These will focus on the motivational conditions in the learning environment.

Experienced learners of languages may be in a position to make a more realistic assessment of their personal learning to date, and to set realistic targets for the next stage in their learning. Those who are inexperienced or returning to learning for the first time after a break, may regard the skills and knowledge that they have developed in other areas of their lives as being irrelevant, or not expressible.

Language teachers know that qualities such as a retentive memory, willingness to take risks and attention to detail are valuable tools to support learning – qualities which can be readily transferred from other fields of human endeavour. We therefore need to develop processes from initial advice, through to curriculum design and delivery, which enable learners to feel that their individual skills and interests are ones which are part of, not separate from, learning. Even more crucially, the ways in which learning achievement is expressed need to provide timely and useful feedback, and be formative – that is designed to help the individual plan the next stages in their learning. A tick on a piece of work, or an anonymous marksheet may motivate some, but will not encourage the individual learner to regard their learning as a process, or feel that their place of learning does either. Nor will it help to give a sense of learning as being something which is integrated into their lives.

In **Leicester Adult Education College** everyone enrolling on a course is given a student handbook. This describes all the college facilities and services available to the learners and what to do to make use of them. In addition, it gives a synopsis of key college policies that impact on learning (Health and Safety; Equal Opportunities) and a clear statement of learner entitlement.

As well as this, learners selecting languages courses are given a range of course information sheets, such as the one below, and are encouraged to complete a self-diagnostic 'test' based on the DIALANG language assessment system which is an application for diagnostic purposes of the Common European Framework (see Appendix, p132).

French Level 1 (03–04)

- *Previous experience/entry requirements*

No formal qualifications or prior knowledge required.

- *Course learning outcomes*

Our courses are mapped against the National Languages Standards and the levels of the European Languages Portfolio. This will enable you to describe your level of competence in the foreign language in a way that is recognised in the UK and in Europe.

This course is for complete beginners. You will gain basic survival and social skills in the foreign language in a variety of situations. You will practise the language covering a selection of topics such as small talk, ordering food and drink in a restaurant, finding your way round town, booking a hotel room, shopping etc.

On successful completion of this course you should be able to: recognise words and phrases you have learned and so make sense of straightforward and simple conversations, instructions and messages; ask questions and give information with help in everyday, familiar situations; understand simple written information; accurately record in writing relevant vocabulary and phrases; identify cultural similarities and differences in the contexts studied; recognise and begin to apply a number of relevant grammatical rules; understand how to use a bilingual dictionary. These outcomes are equivalent to Level 1 of the National Languages Standards and Level A2 of the European Languages Portfolio.

Although homework is not an obligation of the course you will gain greater satisfaction if you are able and prepared to invest some time on study between course meetings. The tutor will suggest how this time may be profitably spent.

- *Teaching methods*

You will be encouraged to play an active part in course meetings. Methods used will include some or all of the following: using the language of your choice with the tutor and other course members to practise speaking and understanding; using audio and video cassettes to help; language games; practising reading and writing skills in class or in self-study; practising grammar through exercises; problem based learning methods; repetition; role-play, small group work, pair work, discussions; demonstrations; making use of ICT.

- *Assessment*

Your progress and achievements may be recognised and assessed continuously in any of the following ways: pre-course diagnostic self-assessment; learner portfolio; learning diaries; set assessment tasks; observed and recorded group activities/role plays; peer observation; self-evaluation forms.

What will learners gain on completion?
Formal qualification achieved will be: optional College Certificate.

- *Progression/next step*

This course provides/supports progression to: Level 2 (first year). We would recommend that at least twenty weeks of study should be completed at Level 1 before you consider a move to Level 2. Other progression options may be discussed with your tutor or the languages co-ordinator.

- *Resources needed*

A4 file, pen, paper, bilingual dictionary; course books/materials etc will be discussed in the first session.

case study

In virtually all settings we are motivated if we are interested in what we are doing, feel that our contribution is valuable and valued, and that we are getting what Rogers terms 'fair reward' (ibid 36) – that is what learners expect from their effort. Where that is not the case, motivation will dwindle and 'may shrivel and die.' (ibid 37). In the languages classroom learners need to feel that they are progressing in a way which is consistent with their expectations – but it is up to us as teachers and providers to find out what these are and help learners plan how to fulfil them. What principles and processes, then, do we need to make this happen and keep our learners motivated?

The face-to-face context

For most adult learners the classroom and their peers become the main focus of their experience and the pivotal element in developing and sustaining motivation. At this level, **a needs analysis** – whether as a paper exercise or arrived at during conversation in the early stages of the course – will help the tutor identify individual learners' motivation, interests and goals and also develop a sense of those which the group has in common, for example leisure activities, travel, music or food. This information will enable the teacher to adjust the course content to sustain motivation, and to encourage student contributions. It is highly advisable that the teacher retains a record of this process in order to monitor how the learner's needs are met throughout the course. Such an approach has the considerable motivational benefit of making learners active participants in the classroom, rather than passive recipients. It is a tangible and genuine acknowledgement of the fact that all learners have lives which extend far beyond the classroom setting and which enrich their contribution to their own learning and that of others.

At the same time as encouraging learners to bring their own wider knowledge and experiences to bear on their learning, the teacher needs to make it clear from the outset that learning is a process which involves discovery and, therefore, scope for mistakes. For many learners the fear of making a mistake can result in an unwillingness to try; in the languages classroom this could take the form of anxious dependence on a dictionary to create pre-prepared responses or a reluctance to speak at all for fear of getting it wrong.

> *It is for the teacher to create an atmosphere where learners feel that they can take risks without diminishing their status.*

In a supportive classroom environment mistakes will be tactfully handled – which is not the same as being ignored! – and the teacher's enthusiasm and genuine interest in each individual and the group is plain to see. It is important to develop linguistic and strategic skills appropriate to individual and collective goals.

case study

An English mother-tongue speaker has a German wife and is learning the language in order to communicate with her family and friends. He also feels that it will help his career in the longer term. He had previously had a dispiriting experience of learning the language at school, in contrast to French, which he enjoyed. He has also picked up Shona informally, and has tried to teach himself Zulu. He cites a sense of progress, and **the teacher's positive and enthusiastic attitude to teaching** as key elements in keeping him motivated.

Dörnyei encapsulates the teacher's crucial role in stimulating and mainting learners' motivation in **10 + 1 commandments**:

1	Set a personal example with your own behaviour.
2	Create a pleasant, relaxed atmosphere in the classroom.
3	Present tasks clearly, giving context and purpose.
4	Develop a good relationship with your learners.
5	Increase the learner's linguistic self-confidence.
6	Make classes interesting.
7	Promote learner autonomy.
8	Personalise the learning process.
9	Increase the learners' goal-orientedness.
10	Familiarise learners with the target language culture.
+1	**Create a cohesive learner group.**

Rogers (ibid: 36) describes what can happen if the tutor does not act as a motivational model:

> '*The class started off with about 20 very keen members. It was a tough course, but the tutor did not help. His analysis seemed remote from the essays we were supposed to do, he talked to the blackboard instead of us; usually only about four other people spoke. Every meeting there was a muddle about which room we were in, so we always started late. By the third meeting people were coming in about an hour late and the group was down to ten. Several people submitted work which they knew was poor, but said they didn't care; one or two people indulged in childish muttering while the tutor was talking – it was a disaster, the whole thing.*'

This is an extreme, and virtually irretrievable situation. There are likely to be much less drastic reasons for erratic or non-attendance. These have chiefly to do with the circumstances of most adult learners' lives: issues such as employment (including variable patterns of employment), family commitments, financial pressures and transport problems. While there is relatively little which we can do directly to help, we can try to minimise the disruption to learning – and therefore possible adverse effects on motivation – which these may cause.

Absent learners

Different institutions have different approaches to dealing with absent students. These may be rooted in long practice or respond to funding body requirements in terms of tracking and recording learner progression through a specified cycle. From the perspective of the class tutor the main point is to consider strategies which will prevent the student who has missed a couple of classes becoming a student who has dropped out for good.

Teachers who keep in touch with students who have missed a class show that they care.

Where a significant reduction in dropout occurs, it is frequently closely linked to students feeling that the tutor was interested enough in them to keep in touch with what was going on in class. Ways of doing this vary and can include a quick postcard, phone call, e-mail (where practicable) or messages letting the student know what has been covered in class, or what has been set for homework.

Motivation outside the classroom

Even in a traditional format, most language learners are likely to have a fairly limited amount of time actually in the classroom. However highly they are motivated while they are there, it is important to support their motivation in between attendances in the classroom.

It is important to consider ways in which students can be encouraged to keep themselves engaged and motivated as autonomous learners.

If we accept the hypothesis that this is most likely to happen when learners feels that their language learning has meaning in their life more generally, then the more we can encourage our students to make their own connections and contributions the better. These could include:

- directing students towards possible resources for self-study, either in their own environment or in an open learning centre;
- penpal exchanges via e-mail;
- students finding out about events relevant to the countries in which the language is spoken.

As what is on offer becomes more flexible in terms of timing, length and manner of delivery, supported self-study and virtual learning environments – including the whole range of possibilities which ICT offers – it is increasingly possible for students to work independently but with guidance, which could include face-to-face teaching, to suit their own needs and circumstances.

Using ICT

ICT/Internet has attracted many learners (often first-time) who are motivated enough to seek out material on-line.

The potential of re-enforcing the face-to-face contact with learners via distance support and self-access outside the classroom, and of using the Internet to bring the world of languages to the students, encourages the learners to take the initiative in extending their learning horizon beyond the classroom.

E-learning – whether through CALL, the virtual classroom, or a rich diet of webcam news in the target language, or through CD-ROMs, discussion groups or chatrooms – is for most learners and teachers a valuable and exciting tool when integrated into traditional learning rather than a total learning experience in itself.

It is essential for learners with no previous access to, or confidence in using ICT to have step-by-step integrated training as part of course design and delivery. This will help them develop the necessary skills and confidence. Equally, institutions should endeavour to train teachers in the use of ICT and its integration into the languages classroom in order to encourage them to make full use of new technologies.

When used in an effective and supported environment, however, on-line provision offers scope for individual learners to find and use material which focuses on their personal needs, is pedagogically valuable and enables them to contribute to the learning community to which they belong (see Appendix, p130).

Developing strategies to address motivational issues

If we accept that meeting students' expectations and keeping them motivated is central to helping them remain enthusiastic and engaged, then what can we do to help? What follows is a summary of the key issues and possible solutions:

- **Matching expectations**: make information as clear as possible. Ideally this should include the strategies and language skills which a learner can reasonably expect to achieve within the time available. Students often find it helpful to be reassured that there will be times when progress feels slower, and that this is part of the learning process.
- **Learning environment**: make it clear by example that all contributions are valid and valued.
- **Learning process**: consider ways in which learners can have, and create, plenty of variety in when and how they learn, and from whom.

This chapter should end as it began, with the learner. The learning age encompasses all of us and it is not a question for us as teachers or trainers whether we participate in it or not, but how much. What motivates and inspires students is seeing that teachers have and can communicate an enthusiasm both for their subject, and for the greater benefits which that subject can bring to the lifelong experience. Let the last word be from a student at the end of a course, commenting on the experience of learning a new language:

I had expected the task of learning this language to be almost impossible and thought originally that I would probably give up after a few weeks. Not so. The teachers recognised what we needed, how each of us learned and until we had all found our feet supported us every step of the way. Then he gave us our heads and in each class we took more and more chances every time. If I had not done it, I would not have believed it possible.

References

Arthur, E. and Beaton, F. (1999) *Adult Foreign Language Learners: motivation, attitudes and behaviours.* Conference paper. CILT Research Forum, March 1999.

Cook, V. (2001) *Second language learning and language teaching.* Arnold.

Davis, G. (2002) 'ICT and modern foreign languages: learning opportunities and training needs'. *Liaison*, Issue 5 (The Language, Linguistics and Area Studies newsletter).

Dörnyei, Z. (1999) *Motivational strategies in the language classroom.* Cambridge Language Teaching Library.

Field, J. (2002) 'Tempting new learners back to the classroom'. *Adult Learning.* NIACE.

Hawkins, E. (ed) (2000) *Thirty years of language teaching.* CILT.

Hogan-Brun, G. (2002) 'Communities and contexts of e-learning in a global age: a plurilingual approach'. *Liaison*, Issue 5.

Jarvis, P. (1995) *Adult and continuing education: theory and practice.* Routledge.

Kelly, M. (2002) 'Crouching strategy, hidden agenda'. *Liaison*, Issue 5.

Marshall, K. (1998) *Why do they do it?* University of Wales Bangor.

Marshall, K. (2002) *Does the truth about languages have to be a state secret?.* UCML.

Nuffield Languages Inquiry (1998) *Where are we going with languages?* (Consultative Report).

Nuffield Languages Inquiry (2000) *Languages, the next generation* (Final Report & Recommendations).

Race, P. and Brown, S. (1998) *The lecturer's toolkit.* Kogan Page.

Rogers, A. (1992) *Adults learning for development.* Cassell.

Rogers, J. (1999) *Adults learning.* Open University Press.

Stern, H. H. (1991) *Fundamental concepts of language teaching.* Oxford University Press.

Tuckett, A. and Cara, S. (1999) *Tongue-tied but trying?* NIACE.

Planning for successful teaching and learning

■ Fiona Copland

This chapter looks at the planning that goes on outside the classroom and at how a specification of a syllabus can be integrated into a scheme of work so that it becomes a teaching outcome in a lesson: in other words, how to interpret a syllabus practically. Throughout this and the following chapter I will be including excerpts from interviews with Frances, an adult learner of Hebrew, Clara, an adult learner of Japanese, and Phoebe, who was until recently an adult learner of Greek and Spanish. These excerpts are included because I feel it is important to have the students' perspective on foreign language learning. I hope that their comments will keep us focused on the importance of the individual learner in our language classrooms.

Defining terms

The words 'curriculum' and 'syllabus' can cause confusion. Generally, the **curriculum** is a reference document specifying overall aims. It 'refers to the totality of content to be taught and the aims to be realised within one school or educational system' (White 1988:4). Curriculum documents for languages generally focus on competence, that is, what a student can do in the language rather than on what the student knows about the language. There are few curriculum documents in existence for modern foreign languages for adults, but the *National Language Standards 2000*, the *Common European Framework for Languages*, and the *Adult Core Curriculum* for ESOL all provide useful generic descriptions of what language students should be able to do in a language at particular levels of ability.

A **syllabus**, on the other hand, is a working document. It details what is to be taught for one particular subject in order for students to progress. As White (ibid) tells us, a syllabus is 'the specification and ordering of **content** of a course or courses'. This means that each level can have its own syllabus, as can each course within this level. For languages, most syllabuses will focus at least on skills and linguistic items that students will need to learn. Some prescriptive syllabuses will tell you how the detailed content is to be taught, but in most cases it is the teacher's job to interpret the syllabus, deciding what items should be taught, when and in which way, recording these decisions in a 'scheme of work'.

The **scheme of work** document details classroom activities, materials, assessment techniques and homework. This can be prepared weekly, monthly or termly, depending on the length and the intensity of the course.

Finally, the **lesson plan** lays out what is to be covered in a particular lesson. Lesson objectives, staging of activities, timing and interaction are included in this document.

The table below summarises these definitions:

Curriculum	the reference document which specifies overall aims of a whole subject area
Syllabus	the content to be covered over a whole term or year of a teaching programme
Scheme of work	a detailed description of what is to be covered over one term/session of the teaching programme, often with activities and homework
Lesson Plan	the content that is to be covered during a particular lesson

From curriculum to lesson plan and back

In theory, we should be able to trace a line from the curriculum document to the activity the learners are working on in the classroom. Let's see if this works.

The **National Curriculum** is the document which sets out what students in British state schools are to learn. In its section on Modern Foreign Languages it states that students should be taught:

> '... knowledge and understanding of **numbers**, quantity, **dates** and time.'

Another competency states that students need to be able to:

> '... **listen for detail.**'

In the Assessment and Qualifications Alliance (AQA) syllabus for GCSE French, these competencies become:

> '... grammar and linguistic structures: **number**, quantity, **dates** and time including use of depuis with present tense;. **Understand** announcements ... **conversations** between two or more people.'

The following scheme of work focuses on particular aspects of this syllabus specification, namely number, months and dates:

Term 3 Week 9			
Topics	*Content*	*Intended Outcomes*	*Resources*
Birthdays	**Numbers 13–31**	Students will consolidate **number vocabulary**.	Number cards
	Months	Students will practise **all months of the year** but will remember months of particular personal importance.	Flash cards Word search
	Dates	**Students will circle the birthday dates they hear the two friends discussing.**	Tape
	Asking and answering about birthdays	Students will be able to ask and answer questions about birthdays.	Survey sheet

There are two one-hour lessons in Week 9. Here is a plan for one of these lessons:

Lesson plan 1	*Name of tutor:* Fantine	*Class:* Level 1 French	*No. in group:* 12	*Date:* 03.03.03	*Time:* 6–7.30pm

Aims: to present and practise months of the year
to provide opportunities for students to memorise these
to encourage students to remember months which are personally important

Extension aims: to give stronger students opportunity to use months of year in sentences with personal relevance

Personal aims: to set the homework in good time rather than in a rush at the end of class!

Topic	**New vocabulary**	**Phonology points**
• Months of the year	• *Janvier*, etc	• Accurate dipthong pronunciation in months such as 'mai'

Language work	**Skills work**	**Anticipated problems**
• *C'est* + month • Mon anniversaire est en _____ • Mon anniversaire de marriage est en _____ • Mon mois préféré est _____	• Identifying months they hear in a listening text. • Matching months with important events.	• Students may get bored with focus on target vocabulary: if this happens, I will introduce some useful phrases such as 'My birthday is in _____', 'My wedding anniversary is in _____', My favourite month is _____.

Time	Teacher's activity	T< >S? S< >S?	Objective	Materials
10 mins	Greetings and social chat.	T< >S	To welcome students. To give ss opportunity to hear and use common French greetings. To demonstrate to students that homework is valued and will be marked.	None.
5 mins	Take in homework (picture labelling activity) and check if learners had any particular problems.	T< >S		
5 mins	Introduce aims of lesson in French and write these on the board.	T< >S	To give learners exposure to natural French. To highlight learning aims for the day.	Board/pen.
3 mins	Distribute cards with months of year. Students, in pairs, try to sort these chronologically.	S< >S	To introduce the names of the months in a supportive way; learners will be able to recognise most of these as they are similar to English months.	Sets of cards with months on.
2 mins	Teacher reads out months in correct order and ss check their cards.	T< >S	To introduce correct pronunciation of the months.	As above.

Lesson plan 1	Name of tutor: Fantine	Class: Level 1 French	No. in group: 12	Date: 03.03.03	Time: 6–7.30pm

Time	Teacher's activity	T< >S? S< >S?	Objective		Materials
10 mins	Pronunciation drill. Teacher holds up flash cards one by one of months. Models pronunciation and ss repeat.	T< >S	To allow ss to practise pronouncing the words in the safety of a group.		Flashcards.
	Then students practise drill in pairs with their cards; one student picks up card and other gives correct pronunciation. (Teacher will monitor and correct ss's pronunciation if required.)	S< >S	To give ss further oral practice.To enable teacher to assess learners' pronunciation.		Small cards.
15 mins	Listening work. Teacher explains to students that they will listen to a conversation between Jean and Marie Claire discussing important dates. First listening: ss listen and tick the months they hear mentioned. (Ss discuss answers in pairs and then feedback). Second listening: ss match the months they hear with the events they represent. (Ss discuss answers in pairs and then feedback).	S< >S	Ss listen and identify months – can they hear them when spoken quickly and in context? Ss listen more intensively to hear if they can match the month to the event.		Listening worksheet. Audio tape.
15 mins	Distribute the transcript of the listening tape. Ss underline key phrases for discussing dates (*Mon anniversaire est en ...*, etc).Teacher elicits these and writes them on the board.	S< >S	Ss see months used in context in key phrases.		Transcript of audio tape.
	Teacher asks ss if there are other phrases concerned with dates that they would like to know. Drill for pronunciation.	T< >S	Ss identify key phrases and practise them orally.		

Lesson plan 1	Name of tutor: Fantine	Class: Level 1 French		No. in group: 12	Date: 03.03.03	Time: 6–7.30pm
Time	**Teacher's activity**	**T< >S?** **S< >S?**	**Objective**			**Materials**
10 mins	Group work. Using the key phrases and months of the year, ss discuss together important dates in their year.	S< >S	Freer oral practice. Learners have the opportunity to personalise the new language through discussing months in relation to their own lives.			None.
5 mins	Feedback. Ss tell class what they found out about others in their group.	S< >T S< >S	Give opportunity to learners to share information and use their French in a meaningful way. Teacher can check accuracy.			None.
5 mins	Set homework – filling in charts about important months in the lives of friends and family for oral practice at the beginning of the next lesson.	T< >S	Integrate homework into classwork.			Chart worksheet.

As you can see, the focus on months in the lesson plan derives from 'months' in the scheme of work, 'grammar and linguistic structures with dates' in the syllabus and 'dates and time' in the curriculum. However, the chain of learning from curriculum to lesson plan is not always hierarchical. What happens in the classroom can result in changes to the scheme of work and even to syllabus and curriculum. If, for example, the teacher finished the class on months and concluded that the twelve months were too many to remember in one session, she might decide to teach the months over a longer period, or even over two different terms. This illustrates the reciprocal relationship between the different planning documents, which is illustrated in the figure below:

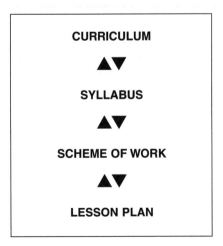

This figure shows that the teacher has an important role to play in the planning process at all levels.

If curricula and syllabuses are to develop and grow, evaluation and input from teachers are crucial.

The syllabus

Many adult learners of modern languages are learning for a variety of personal/professional motivations and there may be no formal curriculum and no imposed syllabus. However, Frances is convinced that having a syllabus is a useful tool, whatever your goals:

> *There is always a tendency that people in a class might put pressure on the teacher...and you might go off on a tangent and not really focus on a specific programme that you have planned ... so if you know that at the end of the day you have to have covered a particular syllabus, that will help you to come back on course.*

Syllabus documents are also useful if courses are to be repeated or replicated. In these cases, documentation helps standardise what is to be taught and learnt.

If you are working at a new centre, or teaching a language that hasn't been taught before, you may find, however, that there is no syllabus document available. Alternatively, you may find that the centre you work in conflates the syllabus and scheme of work into one document. Whatever the case, part of your role may be to write either a syllabus, a scheme of work, or both. This needn't be a daunting task. There are a number of valuable resources that can help you to create these documents. In the following section, we suggest five steps on the path to writing your own syllabus.

Syllabus design

Step 1

First of all, you must decide what your syllabus will cover. As we have seen above, syllabus design is about selecting and grading what is to be taught and learnt. Deciding on categories in which to organisse this content will be the first step in preparing your syllabus document. Here are some categories you could include, depending on the focus of the course and on the needs of your learners:

- topics;
- culture;
- tasks and activities;
- skills (listening, speaking, reading, writing);
- functions (greeting, suggesting, etc);
- situations (ordering drinks, buying stamps, etc);
- grammar;
- pronunciation;
- vocabulary;
- communication strategies (interrupting, starting a conversation, etc);
- learning strategies.

Step 2

Once you have decided syllabus areas, you must decide what **content** will be taught, and perhaps **in what order**. Consulting coursebooks can be useful at this stage, though over-reliance on coursebooks is not advisable. Indeed, there are language departments that teach a considerable number of languages where there are no coursebooks available. In these cases, teachers rely entirely on resources produced over time by the institution or themselves. Coursebooks, certainly for major foreign languages, are piloted and refined so that they aim to meet the needs and level of large numbers of learners. Useful grammar and vocabulary, appropriate to the level, are covered and practice is given in listening, speaking, reading and writing. The 'map' at the front of the book, where topics, language content, skills work and vocabulary are listed, in effect fits White's definition of a syllabus, in that it specifies and orders the content of a course. Selecting from this map according to your learners' needs should help you to develop your syllabus.

Syllabuses that have been posted on websites can also be helpful in deciding content. Looking through what others have selected for their syllabuses can give teachers ideas for their own. Hertfordshire County Council have a particularly good site in this respect, where you can download ready-made syllabuses – called on this site 'curricula' (see Appendix, p132).

Step 3

You then need to present your syllabus as a document, perhaps in a grid. In the syllabus outline below, I have decided to focus on skills, grammar, vocabulary, pronunciation and learner strategies in order to best meet the needs of learners. I then expand on these content areas to suggest what our students will gain from the syllabus (outcomes) and how we are going to measure success (assessment), although the areas of learner and self assessment are covered in more detail later in the book. I have not decided on order of learning as I feel that the teachers working with the classes are in a better position to decide this:

Content	*Outcomes*	*Assessment*
Writing skills Writing short, personal texts	Students will: write a short description of themselves; write a short email to a new chat room friend.	One text written in class with support. One text written outside class.
Grammar Present simple tense Regular and irregular verbs Word order with adjectives	Students will: understand how to form this tense; know to use this tense to talk about habits, states and routines; understand that some verbs are regular and some irregular; understand and be able to use adjectives before nouns.	Two short written texts. Three gap texts. Sorting verbs into regular and irregular groups. Distinguish adjectives from adverbs and order in sentences.
Vocabulary Phrases expressing likes and dislikes	Students will: know and be able to use at least six phrases such as, 'I really like/hate; I can't stand; I absolutely love/hate; I don't mind'.	Two short written texts. Information gap.
Pronunciation Stress in semi-fixed phrases	Students will: say above phrases with correct stress on intensifiers.	Reading texts out loud. Information gap.
Learner strategies Learning vocabulary	Students will: enter phrases in vocabulary notebook under 'semi-fixed phrases'.	Discussion of effectiveness of recording strategy.

Step 4

Before adopting the syllabus, share it, if you can, with your colleagues. They may be able to offer useful suggestions and help you to refine your categories and outcomes. Equally, it may be your line manager's policy to standardise processes and provision and thus encourage you to collaborate on the production of these planning documents and share them for use.

Step 5

Finally, remember that the syllabus is not set in stone. It can be developed, and may need to be, and changed according to what happens in the classroom and according to the individual group of learners in your class. Adjustments such as reducing (or increasing) the content to be covered are normal. Keep your annotated lesson plans (see below) to help you to make adjustments to the syllabus at regular intervals. This strategy will also allow you to review progress towards their learning outcomes with your learners.

Negotiating the syllabus

Another approach to syllabus design is to ask your students what they would like to study overtly within a given framework. **Negotiating** the syllabus with learners has a number of advantages. Spending time at the beginning of the academic year or term with your students, deciding together what should be taught and learnt, puts teachers and learners on an equal footing and suggests to learners that they have as much responsibility for the learning process as the teacher. If you have a class where your students have similar needs (for example, they all want to use their language on holiday in six months' time), then syllabus negotiation should be particularly useful and beneficial. Phoebe, who studied 'holiday Spanish', told us:

> *If you are learning to go on holiday, I would have thought the syllabus should have been determined by the learners themselves, what they want to know and be able to say.*

Nevertheless, syllabus negotiations must be handled sensitively, for the following reasons:

- learners have different needs;
- learners have different learning experiences and levels of prior learning will vary;
- learners have different strengths;
- learners prefer to learn in different ways;
- learners often believe the 'teacher knows best' what they should learn;
- learners may believe that they should follow the coursebook that they have been asked to buy.

Here are some suggestions to help achieve the right balance:

- find out as much as you can about each of your learners. This will help you to select material and activities and to bring in learners' own experiences into the classroom;
- conduct a simple needs analysis at the beginning of the term (see *Learning to learn English* by Ellis and Sinclair and ResourceFile 4: *Mixed-ability teaching in language learning* by Ainslie and Purcell for ideas);

A teacher has to take a balanced approach to the issue of syllabus negotiation if he/she wants to deliver a successful course that involves all learners and appears to favour none.

- share the results of the needs analysis with the learners;
- demonstrate to learners that you are taking account of learning styles and learning needs when you teach (for example, you can say *'Today we are going to look at future tenses because three of you said you were going to book hotels for the summer holiday'*);
- introduce Individual Learning Plans (ILPs) so that learners can work on their own areas of interest/weakness outside as well as inside class (an example of an ILP is given in Chapter 4, p88);
- provide formative assessment as you go through the course, not just at the end. Allocate time to assessment procedures that you can analyse and discuss with your students (this can be: a short test, a piece of writing, a taped conversation; see Chapter 5 for lots more ideas for informal and formal assessment);
- introduce language, tasks, activities that you think will benefit the learners and tell them why; sharing insight into language and methodology is one of the delights of teaching adult learners.

The scheme of work

> *The scheme of work provides details of classroom activities, materials, assessment techniques and homework.*

While it is fair to say that many institutions may not provide syllabus documents for teachers to follow, the majority now will expect teachers to follow standardised schemes of work, which may also be the teachers' responsibility to prepare. As stated above, the scheme of work is a detailed description of what is to be covered over one term/session of the teaching programme, often with activities and homework. As with syllabus design, the first decision you will make will centre on what to include in the scheme.

Pages 44–47 show a scheme of work for a Level 1 French class.

We think that this scheme of work is a particularly useful working document for the following reasons:

- topics and content are clearly stated;
- learning goals are listed in terms of outcomes – it is clear what the students will have learnt at the end of each week;
- resources are given in detail; the teacher will be able to refer to the document in class to find the relevant pages in the coursebook;
- there is the opportunity for the teacher to introduce his/her own material into the class. This leaves space for teachers to make their own contribution to the teaching and learning process, as well as providing variety for the learners;
- assessment has been considered as an integral aspect of the learning process (see Chapter 5 in this book for more on this);
- homework is detailed for each week as an integral part of the planning process, not as an 'add on' at the end of the lesson.

It may be the teacher's responsibility to produce the scheme of work, in which case you need to decide, first of all, whether to write it in English or the target language. Writing it in English increases the document's accessibility: it can be read by students, colleagues, managers and inspectors. Writing it in the target language may make the task itself easier and can also promote ownership and responsibility of the document by the teacher. Before deciding, check the policy and ascertain who will need to see the document.

Scheme of work			French Level 1	Autumn term	
Week	*Topic*	*Content*	*Intended outcomes*	*Resources*	*Assessment activities*
1	Course introduction Revision of Year 1	Greetings Introducing yourself Asking questions Introducing someone else Alphabet Numbers 1–100	Students will be able to: greet someone; give information about themselves; give information about someone else.	Tutor's own selection of relevant material *Façon de parler 1* Units 1–9	Students' responses to tutor's questions Group & pair work activities
2	Revision of personal details Present tense of 'er' verbs	Revision of Week 1 Revision of 'er' verbs	Students will be able to: give information about themselves and others; use the present tense of 'er' verbs.	Tutor's own selection of relevant material *Façon de parler 1* Units 1–9	Students' responses to tutor's questions Pair work activities
3	Revision of present tense of 'er' verbs Present tense of 'faire' Weather	Revision & practice of present tense of 'er' verbs Revision of verb 'faire' Weather	Students will be able to: use the present tense of 'er' verbs; use the verb 'faire'; talk about the weather.	*Façon de parler 1* Unit 10 Tutor's own selection of relevant material	Homework Students' responses to tutor's questions Pair work activities
4	Weather Leisure activities	Talking about the weather Talking about leisure activities	Students will be able to: talk about the weather; talk about their leisure activities.	*Façon de parler 1* Unit 10 Tutor's own selection of relevant material	Homework Students' responses to tutor's questions Pair work activities
5	Leisure activities	Talking about leisure activities	Students will be able to: talk about their leisure activities.	*Façon de parler 1* Unit 10 Tutor's own selection of relevant material	Homework Students' responses to tutor's questions Group and pair work activities
6	Leisure activities Likes and dislikes	Talking about likes and dislikes and leisure activities Adverbs of frequency	Students will be able to: talk about what they like/do not like doing in their free time; say how often they do something.	*Façon de parler 1* Unit 10 Tutor's own selection of relevant material	Homework Students' responses to tutor's questions Group and pair work activities
7	Leisure activities Likes and dislikes Telling the time	Revision of likes and dislikes and leisure activities Adverbs of frequency Telling the time	Students will be able to: talk about what they like/do not like to do in their free time; say how often they do something; tell the time.	*Façon de parler 1* Unit 11 Tutor's own selection of relevant material	Homework Students' responses to tutor's questions Group and pair work activities
8	Telling the time	Revision of time Talking about daily routine and the time at which we do things	Students will be able to: tell the time; say at what time they do various activities.	*Façon de parler 1* Unit 11 Tutor's own selection of relevant material	Homework Students' responses to tutor's questions Group and pair work activities

Scheme of work			French Level 1	Autumn term	
Week	*Topic*	*Content*	*Intended outcomes*	*Resources*	*Assessment activities*
9	Shopping for food	Revision of daily activities Revision of adverbs of frequency Revision of *du/de la/des*	Students will be able to: talk about their daily activities and how often they do them; shop for food using *du/de la/des*.	*Façon de parler 1* Unit 11 Tutor's own selection of relevant materials	Homework Students' responses to tutor's questions Group and pair work activities
10 & 11	Shopping for food Partitive articles	Shopping for food *Du/de la/des* Specific quantities	Students will be able to: shop for food using *du/de la/des* and ask for specific quantities.	*Façon de parler 1* Unit 11 Tutor's own selection of relevant material	Homework Group and pair work activities Students' responses to tutor's questions
12	Revision of first term. Christmas activities	Tradition and customs. Various activities. Revision	Students will revise what they have learnt this term. Students will learn about Christmas traditions in France.	Tutor's own selection of relevant material	Homework. Group and pair work activities. Students' responses to tutor's questions

Scheme of work			French Level 1	Spring term	
Week	*Topic*	*Content*	*Intended outcomes*	*Resources*	*Assessment activities*
1	Revision of first term	Revision of Daily activities Adverbs of frequency Leisure activities Weather Alphabet Numbers	Students will revise what they learnt in the Autumn term.	Tutor's own selection of relevant material	Homework Group and pair work activities Students' responses to tutor's questions
2 & 3	The present tense of 're' verbs. Using public transport.	The present tense of '*re*' verbs. Buying train tickets and enquiring about train times	Students will be able to buy train tickets and ask about train times. They will be able to use '*re*' verbs in the present tense.	*Façon de parler 1* Unit 12 Tutor's own selection of relevant material	Homework Students' responses to tutor's questions Group and pair work activities
5 & 6	At the tourist office.	Enquiring about places to visit and their opening times	Students will be able to ask for information in the tourist office: places to visit and opening times.	*Façon de parler 1* Unit 12 Tutor's own selection of relevant materials	Homework Group and pair work activities

Scheme of work			French Level 1	Spring term	
Week	*Topic*	*Content*	*Intended outcomes*	*Resources*	*Assessment activities*
7	Clothes	Describing what people are wearing Adjectives, particularly colours Materials Sizes	Students will be able to describe what people are wearing.	*Façon de parler 1* Unit 13 Tutor's own selection of relevant materials	Homework Group and pair work activities
8 & 9	Clothes Possessive adjectives	Revision of clothes topic. Possessive adjectives	Students will be able to describe what people are wearing. They will be able to ask for what they want in clothes and shoe shops. They will be able to talk about their own and other people's possessions.	*Façon de parler* Unit 14 Tutor's own selection of relevant materials	Homework. Group and pair work activities
10, 11 & 12	Immediate future with '*aller*' Demonstrative adjectives *Y*	Immediate future with '*aller*' *Ce, cette, ces* *Y* More practice of possessive adjectives	Students will be able to talk about what they are going to do and will be able to use *ce, cette, ces* and *y.* They will be able to talk about their own and other people's possessions.	*Façon de parler 1* Unit 15 Tutor's own selection of relevant materials	Homework. Students' responses to tutor's questions. Group & pair work activities
13	Revision of Spring term	Various revision activities	Students will revise what they have learnt in the Spring term.	Tutor's own selection of relevant materials	Homework. Students' responses to tutor's questions Group & pair work activities

Scheme of work			French Level 1	Summer term	
Week	*Topic*	*Content*	*Intended outcomes*	*Resources*	*Assessment activities*
1 & 2	Travelling by car Present tense of '*ir*' verbs. *Depuis*	Travelling by car. Present tense of '*ir*' verbs *Depuis*	Students will be able to say how long they have been doing something. They will be able to use '*ir*' verbs in the present tense.	*Façon de parler 1* Unit 16 Tutor's own selection of relevant materials	Homework Students' responses to tutor's questions Group & pair work activities
3 & 4	House & home	Furniture & household items *Venir de* Direct object pronouns	Students will be able to talk about their home and household items. They will be able to say what they have just done. They will be able to use direct object pronouns.	*Façon de parler 1* Unit 17	Homework. Students' responses to tutor's questions Group & pair work activities
5 & 6	Present tense of reflexive verbs. Indirect object pronouns *Y & en*	Talking about daily routine Use of indirect object pronouns	Students will be able to use reflexive verbs in the present tense, indirect object pronouns and *y* and *en*.	*Façon de parler 1* Unit 18 and tutor's own selection of relevant materials	Homework Students' responses to tutor's questions Group & pair work activities
7	Introduction to the perfect tense.	Introduction to the perfect tense	Students will start to recognise and use the perfect tense.	*Façon de parler 1* Unit 19	Homework Students' responses to tutor's questions Group & pair work activities

The lesson plan

> *A lesson plan helps you to frame and stage the lesson.*

The lesson plan enables you to think about what you want to teach and how you are going to do so within the framework of your scheme of work. It also gives you time to think about meeting individual needs in the classroom and will give you the opportunity to personalize the content and delivery approach as you get to know the members of your group. For example, have you worked in enough pair and group work for those keen to practise their speaking skills, and is there a focus on vocabulary learning techniques for those who feel that a wide vocabulary is important for their language development?

Lesson plans also provide useful documentation records of the lesson. You can make notes on the plan to show which parts were successful and which not; how long activities actually took rather than how long you thought they would take; and what work you didn't manage to do. This knowledge can feed back in to your syllabus and scheme of work. How and when will you accommodate the work you didn't do? What activities might you rethink given the time it took to do a similar activity today? Do you need to rethink the amount you have planned to cover in the syllabus, given the pace of learning? Filing the plan away preserves a tool for future classes and for future planning. It can help you to plan a better learning experience for your students, and it can save you time!

Who is the lesson plan for?

The lesson plan is primarily for the teacher. Nevertheless, a number of other people may also be interested in seeing your plans from time to time. Your line manager may observe you and will need a copy of the plan in order to follow what is going on. Inspectors are now a normal part of a teacher's life, and they will certainly wish to see plans of the lessons you are teaching. The plans demonstrate to these people that you have thought about the staging and progression of the class, what the learners are going to learn and how they are going to learn it. The plan also provides a document for discussion after a lesson. You can explain why you diverted from the plan in order to meet learners' needs more successfully or demonstrate that certain parts of the plan needed to be further expanded.

You might consider showing your plan to your students. Following the framework for the lesson, students can focus on the progress they are making and can better understand the rationale behind the activities you introduce. At the end of the class, the plan can then be used to evaluate the learning experience and to discuss sections of the lesson learners found particularly useful. Even if you decide not to give students the whole plan, writing the learning outcomes for the lesson on the board will also provide students with a structure for the lesson, and will help them to measure their own learning.

Last, but by no means least, let us not forget that in the day-to-day management non-specialists may need to be able to give information on your lesson to learners who have had to miss a session, or who are ringing in in advance to pass on their apologies. A record of the lesson, either the lesson plan in advance, or at the end of the session, will enable non-specialist staff to give the most appropriate and complete information and advice.

Lesson plan formats

There are lots of different types of lesson plan. Institutions will sometimes insist that all teachers use a particular version but usually teachers are able to choose the one that suits them best. Even very experienced teachers write a lesson plan, although it may not always be as detailed as the Lesson Plan 2, given here:

Lesson plan 2	*Name of tutor:* Pascale Cody	*Class:* Level 1 French	*No. in group:* 12	*Date:* 03.03.03	*Time:* 6–7.30pm

Core aims: By the end of the lesson, students will have:
- learnt and practised eight pieces of vocabulary for labelling what is in the classroom
- practised using *'Qu'est-ce que c'est …?'* and *'C'est une/un …'* to talk about what things are
- scanned a text to identify which items of furniture/equipment are in the room described

Extension aims: More able students will also:
- be given the opportunity to learn more than the core items

Personal aims: I will give the learners enough time to complete the activity today, and will try not to fill silence with talk.

Topic	**New vocabulary**	**Phonology points**
• Labelling things in the classroom	• The cupboard, the whiteboard, *la fenêtre*, the desk, the tape recorder, *le tapis, les murs*	• No 's' sound on plurals • Elision on *'Qu'est-ce que c'est'*

Language work	**Skills work**	**Anticipated problems**
• Oral and written practice of new vocabulary and target forms	• Oral practice asking and anwering questions • Controlled writing practice of target forms and vocabulary • Intensive reading of a description of a room	• There are a number of prepositional phrases in the reading which may worry or confuse students. If necessary, I will provide a key of these phrases on the board

Time	Teacher's activity	T< >S? S< >S?	Student's activity	Objective	Materials
6pm	Welcome students and greet.	T< >S	Listen and greet teacher	Make ss feel welcome. Reinforce 'greetings' phrases.	None
6.05pm	Go over homework (*un or une?*). Monitor while ss discuss.	S< >S	First students check together	Give chance to discuss and feel confident about answers. Identify common problems.	Homework sheet
	Reveal answers one at a time. Focus on answers ss had a problem with.	T< >S	Check answers with OHT	Give clear information about correct forms.	OHT
6.20pm	Introduce eight new words of classroom furniture/equipment. Model and drill pronunciation (chorally and individually). Model and drill full form: *'C'est un/une …'*	T< >S	Listen and repeat	Give ss opportunity to listen to new words plenty of times and to give opportunity to practise these a number of times.	Realia in classroom

Lesson plan 2	Name of tutor: Pascale Cody	Class: Level 1 French	No. in group: 12	Date: 03.03.03	Time: 6–7.30pm

Time	Teacher's activity	T< >S? S< >S?	Student's activity	Objective	Materials
6:35pm	Organise learners into pairs. Distribute sets of labels that ss will stick onto the equipment and furniture.	S< >S	Students work in pairs to label the furniture and equipment in the room. Ss can write new words into vocab note books.	To expose ss to written form of the word. To reinforce the new words. To cater to ss' learning preferences (kinasthetic).	Sets of labels
6:45pm	Ask students to close books. Model new question form: *Qu'est-ce que c'est?* by pointing at labelled furniture around room. Students answer.	T< >S	Ss listen to question form and try to provide answer from memory (can use full or reduced form in answer depending on ability).	To give ss lots of exposure to new question form and to allow them to recall vocabulary words from memory.	None
6:55pm	Set up chain drill to practise new question form.	S< >S	Students sit in a circle. They pass around pictures of items of furniture and as they do so they ask 'Qu'est-ce c'est?' The person on the right answers.	To give controlled practice of new question form and further practice of vocabulary.	Pictures of furniture items
7:10pm	Introduce authentic reading text. **Pre-reading:** ask ss to recall new vocabulary and to add any further items they already know. Introduce new items (with translation) for more able ss.	T< >S	Suggest words.	Recall and expand vocabulary set.	None
	While-reading: ask ss to scan text and to underline all items of vocabulary that they see. Check with partner.	S< >S	Read and underline.	Practise reading skill (scanning) for locating information.	Reading text
	Post-reading: differentiation activities. Weaker students label picture with items found in the text (transfer information). Stronger students answer simple set of comprehension questions.	S	Label or answer questions.	Reinforcement for weaker students and challenging activity for stronger students as they have to extract meaning from authentic text.	Picture of room and set of comprehension questions
7:25pm	Review questions and set homwork – draw and label a room at home.	T< >S	Ask and answer questions.	Give students a sense of achievement and a chance to check learning.	None

As you can see, this plan relates to a scheme of work for French Level 1, week 5. The top of the plan provides **logistics information** about the lesson, which is important for the administration of the centre. Then come the **learning outcomes** for the lesson. The boxes focus on areas that are particularly pertinent to language teaching . Of course, not all boxes will be relevant to all lessons. The columns and rows set out how the lesson will be **staged** and why students are engaged in each activity (the **objectives**). Details such as timing and classroom interaction help the planner to check if there is a variety of activities and a variety of interaction in the classroom. Writing learning outcomes and deciding on interaction patterns and timing will be discussed in detail below. You might like to refer back to the plan given here to see how the descriptions can be interpreted practically.

Completing the plan

Writing learner outcomes

Learner outcomes state what specific new skills and competences the learners will acquire during the lesson.

Mastery of specific new skills and competencies will enable the learner to achieve the overall objectives of the lesson. There is often confusion over the terms aims, objectives and outcomes. Whereas I have put the terms **objectives** and **outcomes** in causal relationship, the **aims** of the lesson can be defined as referring to the teacher's intention as far as the lesson planning goes. The following practical examples show how the three are linked and evolve from a close inter-dependence.

Aims can be expressed in two ways. They can be expressed from the teacher's viewpoint:

To present and practise language for talking about what things are, using 'Qu'est-ce que c'est ...?' and 'C'est une/un ...'

Or from the learner's:

By the end of the lesson, the students will have practised using 'Qu'est-ce que c'est ...?' and 'C'est une/un ...' to talk about what things are.

Teachers can also include outcomes for their own teaching on the plan:

I will give the learners enough time to complete the activity today, and will try not to fill silence with talk.

In our experience, vagueness in lesson outcomes often indicates a lesson has not been thought through. Consider the outcome: ***to practise listening.*** This only gives a very broad indication of what will happen in the lesson and very little indication of what the learners will learn or practise. An outcome such as: ***the learners will listen to a dialogue and identify the order of events in a road accident***, gives a much clearer picture of the point of the listening activity. If this is developed to: ***the learners will listen to a dialogue and identify the order of events in a road accident. Although the dialogue is challenging for this level, learners will only be required to listen for particular pieces of information***, the purpose of doing the activity, to help learners to distinguish useful information from irrelevant information when listening, becomes clear. There are a number of learner outcomes on the plan given here. The first two focus on language development. The third is to develop students' reading skills. You should put your most important outcomes first.

Writing objectives

Each activity we introduce in class should have a purpose. This is the **objective** of the activity. If you find it difficult to articulate the objective for a particular activity, it could be that the activity is not adding anything to the lesson at that point and should be dropped.

Interaction and timing

In many classrooms, the teacher speaks and the students listen and answer the teacher's questions. This approach can be extremely effective, especially when there is a lot of 'content' to be learnt. However, in language classrooms, students need the opportunity to practise what they have been taught. To maximise this opportunity, language teachers plan role plays, pair and group work activities into the lesson.

The **interaction** column in the lesson plan helps us to see at a glance if we have provided these opportunities for interaction. A balance of T<>S (teacher to student) and S<>S (student to student) interaction is what we should be aiming for. S<>S interaction can be introduced in a number of ways without necessarily rethinking the whole lesson plan. For example, students can:

- check answers together at the end of a comprehension activity or listening exercise;
- check their homework together before the teacher goes over it;
- work on new vocabulary together before the teacher explains it;
- work on different questions and then teach each other the answers;
- read out a dialogue together rather than listening to the teacher and another student read it out.

We will come back to pair and group work in Chapter 4 (p86).

Timing is also a planning issue. A common problem is cramming too much into the lesson by becoming overambitious about what is achieveable in the time available, often borne out of anxiety about not offering the demanding adult learner enough substance, enough 'value for money'. Rushing students through activities to get on to the next part can be unsatisfactory for all. When considering timing, two rules of thumb might help:

1 activities generally take longer than you imagine they will;
2 plan an 'if time' activity in case they don't.

> *A good pace keeps motivation high and learners engaged throughout the class.*

The **pace** of the lesson must also be considered when working out timing. When I first started teaching, my trainer advised us to stop activities at their high point rather than allowing them to drift to a ragged finish. This trainer was primarily concerned with keeping the pace up. A more student-centred, differentiated response to the same issue may be to provide **extension activities** for learners who finish the set task quickly, while allowing slower students to complete in their own time. Extension activities should be linked to the activity that the whole class has been working on but should add an extra level of **challenge**. Here are some ideas for extension activities:

- dialogue practice: ask one or both students to try reciting their part from memory, rather than reading it out;
- vocabulary work: ask one of the students to read out definition of a word while the other student/s provide the target vocabulary item;
- gap fill: ask one student to read out the text while the other student, not looking at the text, tries to provide an appropriate word orally;

- text activities: ask students to find five words or phrases they want to learn from the text and write them down.

As you can see, these extension activities do not require the teacher to do any extra work. Instead, teachers exploit the same materials or task in a slightly different way. The links to the original work are then clear to the student, who benefits from extended interaction with the material. Developing such techniques and broadening one's pool of easily employed strategies means that the lesson can be tailored more effectively to varying learner needs and also ensure that the teacher can address what is, more often than not, a **mixed ability** group. The point about differentiation is made at various points throughout the book, but it is worth pointing out at this stage that differentiation tools, as well as core-and-branching, can be applied readily and ensure relevant and personalised language learning in a diverse group of adult learners.

> *Differentiation tools can be applied readily and ensure relevant and personalised language learning in a diverse group of adult learners.*

Post-lesson evaluation

At the end of the lesson give yourself time to go over the plan again, making notes on what was successful and what less so, and making suggestions for improvements. Thinking about your teaching in this way is vital if you want to develop your teaching skills through focusing on strengths and weaknesses. Most institutions of adult education value teachers who are '**reflective practitioners**' and the lesson plan can help make that reflection more focused.

On a more practical level, the practice of 'annotated' leson plans, showing reflection and analysis, can usefully be employed within your department's self-assessment processes as part of your evidence base for all aspects of quality assurance.

References

Ainslie, S. and Purcell, S. (2001) ResourceFile 4: *Mixed-ability teaching in language learning*. CILT.

Council of Europe (2001) *Common European Framework of Reference for languages: learning, teaching, assessment*. Cambridge University Press.

DfES (2001) *Adult ESOL core curriculum*.

Ellis, G. and Sinclair, B. (1990) *Learning to learn English*. Cambridge University Press.

Languages National Training Organisation (2000) *The National Language Standards 2000*. CILT.

White, R. (1988) *The ELT curriculum*. Blackwell.

In the classroom: the teaching and learning process

■ Fiona Copland

The success of the classroom teaching and learning process relies to a large extent on two elements: how you teach and what you teach. In the first section of this chapter we will look at the how of teaching in terms of classroom management. The remainder of the chapter will focus on what to teach, starting with skills work and then moving on to teaching and learning grammatical structures, functions and vocabulary.

Managing the class

One of the key roles for the teacher is as classroom manager. Learners will look to the teacher for decisions regarding who is to speak, what activities are to be done and how these activities are to be organised. Here are a few ideas about how to be an efficient and effective manager of learning:

Encourage participation

- Use eliciting (questioning) techniques to keep the learners involved throughout the lesson (see Scrivener for ideas).
- Learn students' names so that you can nominate quiet or shy learners to contribute to the class discussion when you have developed a comfortable working environment.
- Ask students to write answers on the board, or choose a secretary each lesson to make notes on the board as the class proceeds. Particularly in classrooms equipped with interactive whiteboards this will enable you to produce an accurate and highly tailored record of the particular lesson for a particular class.
- Consider changing the classroom layout: asking students to sit with you in a circle will create a warmer, more intimate environment in which students generally feel more relaxed; asking students to sit round tables in groups will encourage them to communicate with each other as well as with you.

Organise activities

- Give clear instructions, particularly if you are using the target language. Use short sentences, gestures and repetition so that students understand you.
- Demonstrate activities so learners know what they have to do.
- Set time limits so that learners can organise themselves, and monitor the time.
- Have an extension activity ready for those students who finish early.

Provide variety

- Instead of going around the room in orderly fashion, one-by-one, when asking for responses, dot around. Students will listen more intently as they will not know when their turn will come.
- Introduce pair and group work activities to vary the interaction. These activities should provide learners with more opportunity to talk than student/teacher interaction alone.
- Bring in material other than the coursebook. A newspaper article, either in print or taken from the Internet, a television advertisement, some food from the target culture will all be appreciated by your learners.
- Use visual aids, such as pictures, postcards, overheads or maps, to make the lesson come to life.

Use the equipment

- Divide the board into sections. Use one section to record vocabulary that comes up during the lesson, another to record new grammar, and another section as a 'working' section, which you erase frequently to give yourself space. And take care when you write on the board; the students have to look at it throughout the class.
- Use the Overhead Projector. The advantage is that you can prepare work in advance so it will be neater, more organised and more attractive. Use it to 'slowly reveal' information so that learners remain interested.
- Use audio equipment. Play music from your country as learners come into class or when they are working on a piece of writing. Ask students to record themselves; they can later transcribe what they said and work on errors. Show videos of films, TV shows, advertisements from your country, which add a cultural dimension to the classroom experience.
- Use the Internet and other software application as appropriate. We will be looking at the Internet later in the chapter, but there are other applications, such as Microsoft Word and PowerPoint, for presentation phases in a lesson, that allow the teacher to vary media and thus appeal to different learners (and their respective learning styles) at different points in the lesson.

Skills work

Traditionally, skills have been broken down into four areas: listening, speaking, reading and writing. Reading and listening are often referred to as receptive skills as they do not require students to produce any language; speaking and writing are productive skills as they do.

How much time you devote to each skill in the classroom (and for homework) will depend very much on the needs of your learners. Students studying a language for tourism purposes will probably need less work on writing than on listening and speaking. On the other hand, in some examinations, the oral mark is worth considerably less than the grammar section or the reading paper. This will usually have a backwash effect on the speaking component of the teaching and learning programme in that less attention will be paid to speaking.

At this point it might be useful to explain what skills work generally means in language teaching. The focus is on **improving the**

students' ability to perform the skill rather than on presenting or practising new grammatical forms, pronunciation or vocabulary. Language work can be part of this focus, but it is incidental rather than critical. We will see how this interplay between skill and language can work when we consider each skill in detail.

Speaking

For many students, the opportunity for speaking practice is the main reason that they attend the class. Phoebe says:

In my class, there was too much emphasis on writing and not enough on listening and speaking, especially speaking.

Clara reiterates this:

There is not enough opportunity in my class for any sort of extended speaking. I think it would be a good idea if we were encouraged to prepare, for example, a short talk to give in class.

As we suggest above, speaking activities in the classroom broadly fall into two areas:

- speaking to practise new language;
- speaking to improve speaking and interactional, ie. communicative, skills.

The first approach is concerned with improving learners' accuracy in the language. The second approach focuses on improving the fluency of the learners by giving them opportunities to practise what they know. The learners use their language in less predictable ways, without always worrying about trying to include new grammatical features or new vocabulary. Even learners at Level 1 need this kind of practice, and learners at higher levels need more of it. Free practice will help learners to automatise language and use it more confidently. This is the kind of speaking practice that Clara and Phoebe value. Like grammar practice, speaking practice needs to be integrated into the scheme of work and then included in lesson plans, not least to ensure that there is ample opportunity but also integral progression in terms of expectations and competence.

Here are some ideas for fluency activities. The activities at the beginning of the list are suitable for Level 1 students, while those at the end of the list may be best suited to higher level students. However, as the focus here is on the learners using whatever language they know, higher level students should be able to do all the activities:

- students bring in favourite possessions or mementos from trips to the country whose language they are studying, and tell their group about them;
- students discuss in groups what they did at the weekend/what they are going to do in the next holiday/what they would save from their house if it was burning down/where their favourite place in the world is and why etc;
- students prepare a short presentation or talk at home and give it to the class;
- students work together to solve a puzzle in the target language such as a murder mystery or where guests should sit at a dinner party (see Penny Ur's *Discussions that work* for more ideas);

■ students read a newspaper or magazine article and then discuss the contents and give their opinions on the topic.

As you will probably have noticed, these activities all involve learners using language to talk about their feelings or to give their opinions. Adult students generally welcome opportunities to use the language in this way, it makes it relevant and gives the learning purpose.

Organising oral work in the classroom

Giving students a 'reason to speak' can reduce the silences that can fall if we ask students to discuss an issue freely. For example, I could ask students to give their views on 'building housing on greenbelt land'. Many will be happy to do so, but some may not have a strong view or may not be particularly interested in the topic. To improve motivation to speak, I could ask students to list, in order of preference, various plans that have been drawn up for a section of greenbelt land near to where they live. Views will emerge as they discuss, negotiate and decide. It is the ranking activity, however, that gives them the **reason** to speak.

How you organise oral work in the classroom very much depends on the number of students you have in your class. With classes of five or more students can be divided into groups or pairs so that they have more chances to contribute. This may also help students to feel less vulnerable, less inhibited, than if asked to give an opinion in front of the class. Generally, it is best to work through the following stages when setting up oral work:

1   pair/group the students, asking them to sit close to each other and apart from other pairs/groups;
2   explain the activity to the whole class, step by step; if possible, demonstrate the activity. Invite questions in order to check comprehension;
3   distribute any worksheets the learners may need to do the activity (if you give out worksheets **before** explaining the activity, the students will concentrate on the worksheet rather than on what you are saying);
4   set a time limit so that students have some idea how long the discussion is to last;
5   ask students to begin and then monitor unobtrusively in order to check that the groups/pairs are doing what you ask;
6   listen to what the group members say to each other. You may like to join in the discussions, but this is not always necessary. You might decide instead to make notes on content and language use so that you can conduct a useful feedback session (see below) or focus on language errors at the end of the activity;
7   have a feedback session. You can ask for general contributions ('Did anyone find anything particularly interesting?') or ask for solutions to tasks ('So which greenbelt land must never be built on?'). These feedback sessions are best kept short and pacey otherwise students may feel they are only repeating what they have already said.

Social chat

Most classroom interaction does not follow the rules of normal communication. In the classroom, typically, the teacher asks a question, a student answers, and the teacher tells him or her if the answer was correct. In normal conversation, the roles are more balanced, with both speakers asking and answering questions, and little, if any, evaluation of content! Students need the opportunity to practise this kind of chat as well as the classroom interaction they usually have. However, this opportunity is not always forthcoming. Here is a piece of classroom dialogue I recorded recently:

Teacher: What did you do in the holidays?
Student: I went to Scotland.
Teacher: You went to Scotland. Good.

Here the teacher is trying to initiate 'social chat' (*What did you do in the holidays?*) but develops it as 'classroom interaction' when she echoes what the student says (*You went to Scotland*) and then evaluates this (*Good*). A more natural response would have been to comment on the content and ask, for example, if the student enjoyed it or what the weather was like, as in this invented example:

Teacher: What did you do in the holidays?
Student: I went to Scotland.
Teacher: Oh did you? Which part?

It is particularly beneficial for students to be given opportunities for social chat when they are learning the language in their own country, where the classroom will be, for many, the only place to hear and use the foreign language.

Reading

In order to make students better readers, we need to help them to develop reading skills and to give them the opportunity to practise these. Crucially, we need to encourage learners to make choices about how they read texts so that the reading **approach** matches the reading **purpose**.

Students faced with a new text in the foreign language will often try to understand as much as possible by reading slowly and translating new words. This is probably because the student wants to understand the text fully. Furthermore, learners used to texts presenting new vocabulary or grammar will approach all new texts from this learning perspective.

This approach can be inefficient, especially if learners are to take exams in the foreign language or need to cope with long texts. Efficient readers in any language will read according to purpose: they will read a newspaper article in a different way from reading a set of instructions in a recipe. Sophisticated readers who are aware of different reading approaches are able to transfer the skill from one language to another. Less sophisticated readers are not and therefore need the teacher's support in developing the skills.

Reading skills

Some reading skills that we can teach learners are given below. As with the activities in the speaking section, those at the beginning of the list are suitable for all levels, while those towards the end may be better suited to higher levels.

- **scanning** – this is when we read **to find out particular pieces of information**. If I want to look at my newspaper article again to find out when or where the story took place, for example, I would scan through the text to locate these particular pieces of information. You may be reading this chapter in this way, looking through quickly until you find the section on reading. Scanning is a useful skill to present to Level 1 and Level 2 learners so that they become confident about approaching texts of all lengths and levels of difficulty;

- **intensive reading** – this is when we read **to understand as much as possible** about the text. You may be reading this chapter intensively, trying to assimilate information and rereading sections that do not make sense to you the first time. Learners at all levels need to work on decoding meaning in this way;

- **skimming** – this is when we read to get the **gist** of a text. If I read a newspaper article, I generally skim through to get a good idea of the story or the ideas presented. I read quickly and without worrying if I have understood everything. After skimming a text, I could give a brief summary of what I have read, but may not be able to remember details. This skill is useful for students, especially at Level 3 and above, as their language Level should enable them to understand a good amount of the grammar and vocabulary of general interest texts;

- **making inferences** – this is when you read and **make a judgement** on what you have read. Was the text written in an ironic way? What opinion did the writer of the piece give, and did you agree? These skills can be practised from Level 2, although learners at higher levels will find them less daunting;

- **extensive reading** – this is **reading for pleasure**. When I read a novel I read in this way, or when I read a magazine article. I am reading for the pleasure that reading gives me; I am not primarily concerned with explicitly learning new things. Learners at all levels should be encouraged to do this, although realistically, it is higher level learners who will generally get pleasure from reading in the foreign language.

Putting the theory to work

Pages 60–61 show a lesson plan for a Level 3 English lesson. It shows how the purpose of the reading determines the choice of activities, and how activities are integrated into bigger activities that allow the learners to follow the rationale and the gradual build up of confidence and competence. The lesson was developed by Raymond Sheehan, who teaches English in the United Arab Emirates. Raymond's overall aim is to develop learners' reading confidence and skills so that they are able to read authentic (real life) texts successfully.

The students are reading a newspaper article about a young German's cycle ride through the city of his birth. The photo shows Florian Schulz on his bike in Abu Dhabi.

Cyclist on epic journey

TRAVEL
———

Twenty-one years after his birth at the Abu Dhabi Corniche Hospital, Florian Schulz is back in the emirates on a cycling expedition that has seen him pedal from his home in Germany to the emirates.

Today will be five months to the day since Schulz hit the road on an epic journey that will end in South Africa

Lesson plan 3	Name of tutor: Raymond Sheehan	Class: Level 3 English		No. in group: 12	Date: 03.03.03	Time: 6–8pm

Aims: to encourage the learners to read an authentic text for gist (skimming);
to encourage students to build up their understanding of the text by reading to find out specific information (scanning);
to encourage learners to guess the meaning of words in context;
to encourage learners to reflect on their achievement in accessing the text.

Personal aims: I will spend time at the beginning of the lesson leading into the text and raising students' interest in the text before they read.

Topic	**New vocabulary**	**Phonology points**
• Cyclist on an epic journey	• 'To the day', 'hit the road', 'generous', 'ferry', 'yacht'	• Pronunciation of place names

Language work	**Skills work**	**Anticipated problems**
• It is + complement	• Scanning for specific information • Inferring meaning	• Students may feel discouraged by the length of the text • Activities may take longer than planned

Time	Teacher's activity	T< >S? S< >S?	Student's activity	Objective	Materials
6pm	Welcome students and discuss what they did at the weekend.	T< >S	Listen and answer questions.	Introduce an element of 'social chat'. Demonstrate interest in learners.	None
6.10pm	Ask students what their favourite kind of transport is and why. Ask ss to label pictures of ferry, raft and bike.	T< >S	Discuss favourite types of transport. Label picture.	Raise interest in the topic. Check ss know key vocab.	Pictures to label
6.20pm	Hold up the article the students are going to read. Distribute pre-reading questions: 1 Do you think this is from a newspaper or magazine? Why? 2 Look at the picture, what do you see? Where is he? 3 Look at headline. Which two words can you connect to the picture? What is a cyclist? 4 Guess the meaning – **epic** and **journey**	S< >S	Look at text and answer the prereading questions in pairs.	Students interest in topic further engaged. More important vocabulary introduced. Context set for reading text (Cyclist in Abu Dhabi).	Set of questions

Lesson plan 3	*Name of tutor:* Raymond Sheehan	*Class:* Level 3 English	*No. in group:* 12	*Date:* 03.03.03	*Time:* 6–8pm

Time	Teacher's activity	T< >S? S< >S?	Student's activity	Objective	Materials
6.45pm	Set while reading tasks: 1 Underline all the names of countries 2 Classify the countries:European/ Non-European 3 In what order did he visit the countries? List them in order.	S S< >S	Complete tasks, first individually and then in pairs.	To introduce scanning activity to students. To enable students to extract some useful information from the text despite their limited reading skills.	
7.00pm	Check answers and then set next reading task: complete immigration form with details of the cyclist.	T< >S S< >S	Suggest answers. Work in pairs to complete immigration form.	Students continue to extract limited amounts of information from text. Integrate reading and writing.	Immigration form
7.20pm	Set short comprehension questions.	S S<>S	Students answer questions independently and then check with partner. (NB Stronger students can attempt this without consulting the text.)	To check basic understanding of text. To give all students a sense of achievement at extracting information from the authentic text. To provide stronger students with a greater challenge.	List of comprehension questions
7.35pm	Check answers on power point. Set Vocabulary activity.	T<>S Groups	Check answers. Ask for clarification. Students work in groups to complete vocabulary activity.	To check understanding. Group work for variety of interaction. Also, ss can help each other.	CD Vocab worksheets
7.50pm	Check answers. Set memory multiple choice game.	T<>S Groups	As above, in pairs, ss work in competition with each other, to see which group can remember most.	To demonstate to students how much they have understood. To introduce a fun element at the end of a challenging class.	CD Multiple choice task.

This lesson plan gives learners practice in a number of reading skills. In its staging, it provides a useful framework for reading and listening lessons – pre-reading work; while reading work; and post-reading work. These stages are discussed below:

Pre-reading

As you can see, the first activities the learners do are not text-based. Instead, the teacher is **leading into the text** to develop the learners' interest in the subject and to motivate them to read it. In our opinion, this stage is crucial to a successful reading lesson. The students will be 'warmed up' and will have a good idea what the reading text will be about. **Pre-teaching vocabulary** that learners need to understand the gist of the article follows the warm-up phase.

While reading

The first reading activity is a **scanning** activity. Students search for names of countries that the cyclist travels through. This activity gives learners an overall understanding of the cyclist's journey without having to read the whole text.

The second reading activity involves scanning and also intensive reading. This time the students are presented with a set of **comprehension questions**. Some of these are literal, some inferential and some personal response type questions (see below, this section).

Finally in the 'while reading' section, the students do a **vocabulary activity** to encourage them to guess meaning from context and to develop their personal vocabularies.

Post-reading

The students are asked to put the text away and to respond to a multiple-choice activity based on the content of what they have read. The students should be able to answer these questions easily, demonstrating to them that it is not necessary to read the whole text to get both the main points of the story, and some useful detail.

You can use the Pre-reading, While-reading and Post-reading design criteria to structure reading (and listening) lessons. Nuttall's *Teaching reading skills in a foreign language* and Grellet's *Developing reading skills* provide ample ideas for developing each of these stages.

Asking questions

Comprehension questions are a common technique for checking if learners have understood the meaning of the text. They can be asked and answered orally or in written form. They can be open-ended questions (How? Why? When? What? Where?), Yes/No questions (Did/Do?) or multiple choice. Christine Nuttall has classified five types of comprehension question. These are listed below with illustrative questions based on the bicycle text given above:

1 *questions of literal comprehension*: the answers to these questions can be found 'directly and explicitly' (ibid) in the text. For the bicycle text, a literal question might be: 'Where did Florian start his journey?'

2 *questions involving reorganisation or reinterpretation*: the student finds the answer to these questions by finding information in the text which is given in a different way to how it is expressed

in the question, or by gathering information from different sections of the text;

3   *questions of inference*: this is a sophisticated question type. The learners must 'consider what is implied but not explicitly stated' (ibid). An example of a question for our text might be: 'Which country do you think Florian has enjoyed most on his journey?'

4   *questions of evaluation*: this is a reader response question. The students can be asked if the piece is biased in any way or if the piece is well-written;

5   *questions of personal response*: this is another reader response question. This time the students are asked to respond to the content of the text, for example, 'Would you like to travel across land like Abu Dhabi? What kind of transport would you choose?'

When asking or writing comprehension questions of your own, this classification provides a useful checklist. Of course, you don't always have to include each type of question, and they don't need to be grouped together at the end of the text (you could ask type 1 and 2 questions after the first reading, for example). You can also use this checklist to evaluate questions in your coursebook: is there a balance of question type, or are the questions only aimed at extracting information from the text?

Reading interactively

Reading can become an 'interactive' activity, involving speaking and listening, if learners are required to share what they have read with each other. The activities listed below require students to practise reading skills, but also encourage interaction. The first two activities can be used with all levels while the last two activities are usually successful with higher level learners:

- **transferring information**: this is a scanning activity. Students look through a text for key information and transfer this to a table. For example, students can scan through a text which gives biographical details about a number of people to find information such as age, occupation, hobbies, which they then use to complete a table for comparison. Students can collect different information and then share, or the same information, which they can then check with each other;
- **reordering the text:** this activity requires learners to read intensively. Texts which have a strong narrative line can be cut up and given to students to reorder. Students have to work out how the story unfolds and be aware of discourse markers such as conjunctions in order to be successful at this task;
- dividing the text among students (**jigsaw reading**): here students read a section of the text intensively and then summarise what they have read. Each student is given a section of text which he/she reads through, using a dictionary to check that he/she understands it well. Each student then tells the other students in the group about his/her text. When all students have summarised their texts, they discuss how they think the text is organised, in other word, whose text is first, second, third etc;
- **creating an information gap:** you can use information gaps to make a reading task interactive. Students work in pairs. Each student has a different half of one text and a set of questions which are only answered in his/her partner's text. Students read their own half and then ask their partner their questions in order to build up a complete picture of the text as a whole. At the end, students can read their partners' texts to see how much they have understood from the information exchange.

Listening

For many students learning a foreign language in Britain the best opportunity they have to listen to the foreign language is when the teacher talks to them. This is a strong argument for using the target language as much as possible in the classroom, especially when we consider that many researchers believe exposure to 'comprehensible input' to be the most important factor in acquiring the target language (see Krashen, Ellis). This might not be as easy as it seems, however. Level 1 and Level 2 learners can find that too much classroom talk in the target language is both tiring and frustrating. Teachers can struggle, for example, to explain a new word in the target language, when a simple translation would be more efficient. Successful target language use relies on a number of factors:

- teachers have to **grade their language.** This means that the teacher must consider the level of complexity the learners will be able to cope with. With Level 1 learners (and to some extent Level 2), teachers need to use simple sentences and monitor the use of idiomatic language, which can often be more troublesome for learners than more formal forms;
- teachers will, in some cases, need to **slow down.** There is a balance to be drawn here between a speed that learners can tune in to accumulatively, and a slow parody of natural language use;
- **classroom management phrases** can be delivered in the target language as they are often repeated. In Japanese, *'Futtari kudasi'* means work in pairs, a phrase I picked up at an observation of a Level 1 group through hearing it again and again;
- teachers have to learn to **recognise fatigue** in their learners and break from target language use when appropriate;
- teachers should try not to use a pigeonised version of the target language with their learners as this gives students a model of the target language which they will not hear elsewhere.

Teachers can, of course, provide other forms of listening practice in the classroom so that learners hear a variety of voices and accents.

Listening skills

Most coursebooks have an accompanying tape or CD. The texts on these tapes have a number of functions:

1 to present new language structures and vocabulary;
2 to present functional language, such as inviting and suggesting;
3 to model pronunciation;
4 to help learners to practise listening skills.

In this section, we will primarily be concerned with skills development.

As with reading, learners can be helped to listen more effectively through giving them practice in different listening skills.

- listening for gist (skimming);
- listening for specific information (scanning);
- listening intensively;
- listening extensively.

As you can see, these listening skills equate very broadly to reading skills and so we will not repeat ourselves by describing them in detail. Instead we will give an outline of a listening lesson designed to improve the first two skills.

Putting the theory to work

The steps involved in setting up a listening skills lesson also resemble those for setting up a reading lesson: usually there is a pre-listening, while-listening and post-listening phase. These stages are clearly laid out below:

Before the lesson starts, make sure the tape recorder is working; that the tape counter is on zero; that the speaker is facing towards the learners and that the sound level is at a reasonable level.

Pre-listening

Before playing the tape, spend some time setting what the learners will hear in context; after all, the students will have no visual clues to help them to work out what is going on.

Teach any vocabulary that is essential for the students' understanding of the listening text and tell them about the tape – you will hear two people, a man and a woman – for example.

While listening

Then set a gist question, or a simple task that will help the learners to tune in to the tape.

Play the tape, ask students to check their answer together and then elicit the answer to your question.

Before playing the tape again, ask a few general comprehension questions (but avoid specific ones such as 'What word is used to describe ____', which can be demotivating). Give students time to answer (count to ten if necessary!).

Set a task which relies on the learners listening for specific information; this might be a set of comprehension questions; a gap-fill activity; an ordering activity or note-taking, for example. Before playing the tape, allow the students to become familiar with the task by giving them a few minutes to read through (and perhaps answer some of the questions).

Play the tape again. Ask the students to check their answers together, and then elicit the answers from the whole class.

Now ask some detailed comprehension questions.

Post-listening

Do some work on the listening text. One idea is to ask students to listen again but with the tapescript so that they can listen to how the words and phrases on the paper are pronounced. (It is the pronunciation of the words and phrases rather than the meaning that is often a barrier to understanding: the students can understand the words if they see them written down, but can't decipher them when spoken at speed, where sounds change or even disappear.) Another idea is to ask students to underline five phrases from the text that they want to learn.

There is no doubt that many students find listening to tapes extremely difficult: I recently heard one sympathetic native speaker teacher of Spanish encourage her learners by telling them not to worry too much about understanding the tape as she remembered how hard she had found listening activities of this kind when she was learning English.

Learners do need support when listening: short chunks of text are best and giving learners time to process what they have heard is also helpful. Here are some approaches and strategies for working with audio materials:

- ask students to predict what will happen on the tape before they hear it;
- stop the tape before the end and ask students to guess what happens;
- pause the tape on the second or third listening to give learners time to process the information that they hear;
- distribute the tapescript and ask students to follow as they listen. Students can then focus particularly on parts of the tape that they didn't understand, and decide if the misunderstanding arises from the grammar, vocabulary or pronunciation of the phrases;
- jigsaw listening. Instead of reading different sections of text (as described above) students listen to different sections of tape and then share information. You will need more than one classroom if you wish to do this, or good headphones!

Video

Videos can be easier for learners to understand than tapes as the context is provided and visual clues help with meaning. Learners generally like video work, too; the entertainment function can predispose them to approaching video work positively.

A listening/viewing lesson to improve skill can, in many instances, follow the outline given above. However, as the visual aspect is important to access meaning, try to avoid giving learners too many written exercises, certainly at the first 'viewing'.

Here are a number of strategies you can employ with video:

- play the video tape with the sound off: learners can guess what the video is about and what the characters are saying;
- ask the learners to sit back-to-back so that one student can see the screen and the other can't. With the sound down, the student facing the video gives a running commentary of the action. The other students can ask as many questions as desired;
- learners act out what they have seen on the video;
- give learners the video script and ask them to practise 'shadow talking'. This is when the students say the words at the same time as the actors on the screen. This technique can help students particularly with pronunciation, intonation and stress.

Guest speakers

If you are teaching a language outside the country where it is widely spoken, it is probable that your students have few chances to practise the language outside the classroom. Interaction with expert or native speakers will perhaps be limited. Inviting a guest speaker into your class can give your learners useful practice opportunities, and can boost their confidence.

Guest speakers can either come in to the class to present something –
slides, something cultural, etc – or can take the 'hot seat' and be
interviewed by the students. Either way, lessons before the visit should
be spent in preparation, learning vocabulary, preparing questions and
practising listening skills.

Writing

For many learners, writing in the foreign language is not particularly
important. These learners are learning in order to communicate orally
in the target language and to read documents such as menus and other
tourist literature. I will discuss writing activities for these learners in
the first part of this section.

Other learners need to perform a number of written tasks in the
foreign language, for example, writing e-mails, writing notes or writing
to friends. For students taking examinations, being able to produce
longer texts which communicate effectively is an extremely important
skill. I will discuss writing activities for these learners in the second
part of this section.

Finally, learners in both these groups may be writing in a different, i.e.
non-Roman script. This will be discussed in the third part of this
section.

Controlled writing

Writing is a useful technique for consolidating language learnt in the
classroom. Clara told us:

*I love the writing homework. It is quite often totally
mechanical, things like having a huge chunk of verbs
and then you have to put them in the gaps, but I really
enjoy it.*

Introducing writing is also an effective way of getting a variety of
activities into the classroom, an approach which many students
appreciate. For these reasons alone, it is worth planning writing into
your scheme of work, whatever the skills needs of the learners.
However, the learners' needs and preferences should dictate the type
of writing activity you introduce and the frequency with which you do
so. For learners who are not strongly motivated to improve writing
skills, controlled writing will fulfill the criteria of consolidation and
variety without alienating learners.

Controlled writing supports learners by providing structures and
vocabulary to help them to write successfully. Here is a selection of
controlled writing activities which are probably most suitable for lower
level learners:

Gap fill

The most controlled writing activity is the **gap fill**, where students
need only write a word or short phrase into a space. Gap fills are most
often used to give learners practice in grammatical items or in new
vocabulary. The level of difficulty can be controlled in a number of
ways. In the gap fill activity below the words are gapped regularly –
every seventh word in this case – and learners have no guidance for
completing them. This is called a **cloze** text:

This chapter is about teaching adult _____. We hope you are enjoying it _____ that it has answered some of your _____. At present, we are discussing writing _____ , in particular controlled writing activities. The _____ section is about helping students to _____ longer texts.

Cloze texts test learners' overall knowledge of the language. In the text above, students have to understand sentence structure if they are to complete the gaps successfully.

There are other types of gapped exercises which can give learners more support. For example:

- gap only one type of word (for example, verbs);
- provide the words that fit the gaps in a box at the top of the gap fill text;
- provide the word to fill the gap after the gap; students must decide on the correct **form** for the word (tense, plural, determiner etc);
- provide a choice of three words for each gap; learners try to choose the correct one;
- use spaces to gap the word; learners then know how many letters each gapped word has.

In a mixed-ability class, gap fills with different levels of support can help learners to achieve the task at their own level.

Pattern drills

Students write a number of sentences following the same linguistic pattern, as in the example below:

Imagine you won three million pounds on the lottery next weekend. How would you spend it? Write three sentences. Here is an example:

If I won three million pounds, I would buy a large house in southern Italy.

In a similar vein, jumbled sentences encourage learners to focus on syntax as they rewrite the sentence correctly:

three   if   pounds   won   million   I   ,   in   southern   Italy would   a   house   buy   I   large

Students can find producing controlled writing of this type satisfying. They know that what they have produced is largely accurate and they can feel that repeating the structure will help them to internalise it. When learners are also learning a new script, intensive practice of this type is often particularly welcome.

Other controlled writing activities include:

- expanding a text – students are given the bare bones of a text and have to expand it to make a coherent whole;
- stem sentences – students are given the first half of a sentence and have to complete it, for example, **I love Paris when ...** ;
- writing notes – students write and answer notes to each other with the teacher acting as post person. This is especially effective for practising invitations/acceptances/ refusals, or for suggesting things;

■ consequences – students write one line of a story and then pass their paper on to the person sitting to their right. They then write a contribution to the story they have received by writing a new line.

Personalising controlled writing activities

In the pattern drill practice above there is an element of personalisation as learners are asked to use the language form (if + past simple + would) to express their own wishes. This kind of controlled writing practice has the advantage of engaging learners at the level of meaning as well as form. Personalising activities in this way appeals to Clara:

I quite like being able to practise in a more personal way language structures we've been working with but often it's not personal enough ... it is often based on other people's opinions about what they like to eat, for example.

Phoebe has had similar experiences:

All I can remember is how to order one cup of coffee with sugar in it, and I don't even take sugar!

Personalising an activity will often require no preparation and little more than a change of instruction. In the following activity learners are asked to note down the likes and dislikes of a character in a coursebook:

Le gusta (n)	No le gusta (n)
la música	
los libros	
el fútbol	
la bicicleta	
la familia	
las películas	

To personalise the activity, the teacher could ask learners to write down whether they like or dislike these things.

Me gusta (n)	No me gusta (n)
la música	
los libros	
el fútbol	
la bicicleta	
la familia	
las películas	

The teacher could then interview learners while the others listen and note down what their classmates like and don't like. Students could then interview the teacher and each other to practise the question forms as well as the answers.

Extended writing

For students who have to write longer pieces of text, two things are crucial: exposure to the kinds of text they have to produce; and plenty of opportunities to rework and correct their own texts as they produce them. These two elements are often called **product** and **process**. I will discuss each in turn.

Writing as product

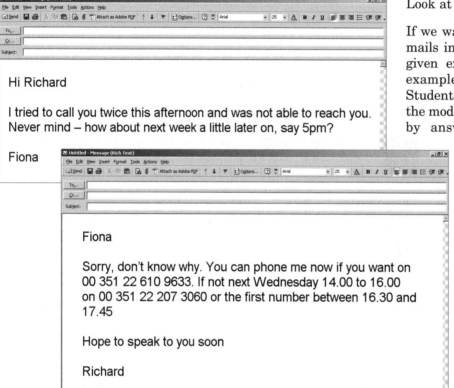

Look at these two e-mail messages.

If we want our learners to write e-mails in this style, they need to be given examples to look at. These examples are called **model**s. Students can be asked to work with the model by filling gaps in the text, by answering questions on the content and then by producing a similar text themselves. A problem with this approach, however, is that students can feel that they need to copy the model exactly; another is that they may feel disheartened by the challenge of achieving native speaker writing competence.

One way of focusing on writing as product is to find **generic features** that the target texts share. These e-mails, for example, share a number of features: they are short; they are informal; they use shortish sentences; greetings are minimal. You can draw students' attention to these generic features through guided questions. Questions you could write for these e-mails include:

1 How do the e-mails start?
2 How do they end?
3 Are the messages formal or informal?
4 How many sentences are in each e-mail?
5 How many words are in each sentence?
6 Who is going to read the messages? What is his/her relationship to the sender?
7 What do both senders know about writing e-mail messages?

Learners then have a number of guiding principles to help them to write their own e-mail messages. Usually a group of four or five texts written for a similar purpose is enough to get evidence of the basic features the texts share. Features to look for include:

- length;
- audience;
- purpose;
- how the information is organised;
- how the texts begin;

- how they finish;
- specialised vocabulary.

Writing as process

Adult learners can become anxious about writing at length, not least because it may remind them at times of experiences of writing at school where the purpose was not always clear and where writing activities seemed to have been taken out of context. In addition, adult learners may be worried because of the inherent, and more formal, element of scrutiny to their work: their writing can be read by others, and can therefore be judged. Process writing is concerned less with the final written text than with how the texts are written. Focusing on the process of writing can lessen anxiety for learners as opportunities are given to draft and redraft the text; texts become work in progress rather than finished products. A process writing activity is staged in the following way:

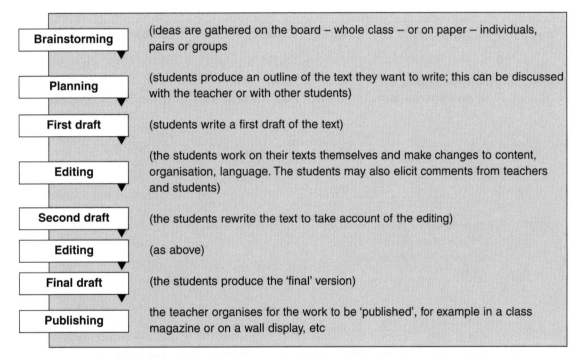

Brainstorming	(ideas are gathered on the board – whole class – or on paper – individuals, pairs or groups
Planning	(students produce an outline of the text they want to write; this can be discussed with the teacher or with other students)
First draft	(students write a first draft of the text)
Editing	(the students work on their texts themselves and make changes to content, organisation, language. The students may also elicit comments from teachers and students)
Second draft	(the students rewrite the text to take account of the editing)
Editing	(as above)
Final draft	(the students produce the 'final' version)
Publishing	the teacher organises for the work to be 'published', for example in a class magazine or on a wall display, etc

A great deal of effort needs to be put in by teachers and learners for process writing to be successful. The main benefits are that the learner 'finds' his/her own 'voice' during this process, rather than being given a voice to imitate (a criticism sometimes made of the product approach). The learners often produce good quality work and develop their personal grammar and vocabulary through the editing process. If you want to find out more, *Process writing* by Ron White and Valerie Arndt is a good place to start. A disadvantage of this approach is that it can take a lot of time. There is also the possibility that the text the learner produces would not be recognised as being typical of the text type to which the learner aspires. Many teachers find that they are able to achieve good results by integrating techniques from the process and product approach.

Integrating process and product

In our fourth lesson plan, the strengths of process and product are combined to give learners opportunities to draft and redraft work, at the same time as knowing what kind of text they are aiming for.

Lesson plan 4	*Name of tutor:* Penny Burgess	*Class:* Business writing (Level 3)	*No. in group:* 10	*Date:* 14.08.03	*Time:* 8–10pm

Aims:	to raise students' awareness of generic features of semi-formal e-mail messages; to provide students with a useful model for this kind of writing; to give students an opportunity in class to practise writing this kind of message; to encourage students to plan and to edit their writing.
Personal aims:	I will try to foster a supportive learning environment so that students feel comfortable sharing their work and offering constructive comments.

Topic	**New vocabulary**	**Phonology points**
• Semi-formal e-mail messages	• *Genre* and *generic*	• *Genre* and *generic*

Language work	**Skills work**	**Anticipated problems**
• Constructing accurate short sentences	• Drafting and editing an e-mail message	• Ss may not want to rewrite the message. I will encourage them to do this by offering to respond if they send the corrected version to me.

Time	Teacher's activity	T< >S? S< >S?	Student's activity	Objective	Materials
10.00	Introduce topic for the day and write the aims on board.	T< >S	Listen and write down aims if appropriate.	Students understand learning outcomes for the lesson.	
10.10	Distribute e-mail messages on card to ss in groups.	S< >S	In groups, ss sort messages into formal, informal and semi-formal.	To introduce importance of audience and tone when writing e-mails.	Sets of e-mail messages.
10.25	After checking answers, elicit main features of informal e-mails. Write on bb.	T< >S	Suggest features.	To work from what students know of target genre.	
10.35	Distribute e-mails 1 and 2 and set of questions to ss in pairs.	S< >S	Students work together to answer questions.	Discovery learning. Students work together to discover features of target genre.	E-mails 1 and 2 and questions.
10.45	Feedback. Add to list of features on board.	T< >S	Suggest further features based on pair work activity.	Students have full list of important features of target genre.	
10.55	Set writing task. Ss to respond to e-mail 3 in semi-formal style.	S	Students produce first draft of e-mail replying to e-mail 3.	Students practise producing own e-mail focusing on target features.	None
11.15	Set pair editing task.	S< >S	Students swap emails. They then read their partner's email and decide if the emails contain the target features. Discuss findings with partner.	Students discuss strengths and weakness of first draft of e-mail.	E-mail 3
11.30	Set up rewriting task.		Students write second draft of e-mail message onto overhead projector transparencies.	Students try to improve their writing and publish their final version.	Transparencies

Literacy issues

Greek, Hebrew and Japanese all have different scripts to English, yet this has not daunted our three learners. The Greek alphabet is arguably the easiest, and Phoebe found the learning process relatively unproblematic:

 We learnt the upper case alphabet one week and the lower case alphabet the next. It came quite quickly.

Japanese, on the other hand, combines three different scripts in written text, and successful readers and writers must be competent in all three. Clara felt that understanding the *kanji* – the Chinese characters used in Japanese – was not taken seriously in her class:

 Even when I joined a Level 3 class I found we were not being taught anything whatsoever about kanji, and I felt that this was awful, quite frankly.

So awful, in fact, that she gave up her classes for a year to teach herself this written form.

For all three learners, reading the new script was essential; writing was desirable. They believe that students should be exposed to the new scripts from the beginning so that reading developed alongside speaking and listening skills.

Teaching new scripts from the beginning also makes sound pedagogic sense. You can take advantage of the students' motivation and willingness to invest time, which are generally apparent at the start of a new course, and set learning the scripts as homework tasks. The sense of achievement and steep progression which accompanies success at this task will hopefully motivate students further. The new reading/writing skills should also have a positive influence on what and how the students learn: authentic texts in the target script, be they in print or electronic formats, now become available to them and independent learning is given a boost.

Most learners agree that when learning new scripts 'little and often' is the key. There are lots of fun activities you can give students to work on in class to practise and review this aspect of language. Here are a few ideas for learners beginning to learn a new script:

- **play word/character bingo**: students prepare their own bingo cards by choosing, for example, six out of thirty characters that are available and writing them in individual squares on their bingo cards:

ρ	α	π
σ	μ	ε

The teacher then gathers up the thirty characters and either says or shows them in turn to the learners. The first person to see/hear all their characters wins by shouting 'bingo!'.

- **pelmanism**: this is a matching activity. Students are given sets of cards. On some cards are pictures and on some cards are characters/letters. These cards correspond to each other (for example, the object on the picture card begins with one of the letters on one of the letter cards). The cards are spread out face down and students take it in turns to turn over two cards at a time. If they get a matching pair, they keep them.
- **anagrams**: letters are jumbled up and students reorder to form the word.
- **hangman**: the teacher (or a student) writes up a number of spaces on the board corresponding to letters/characters that the learners know. Students take it in turns to shout out letters/characters to try to guess the word. If they guess correctly, the teacher writes it in. If not, the teacher begins to draw a 'hanged man', one limb for each incorrectly guessed letter/character.

If learners do need to learn a new script when learning the language, it is likely that their literacy skills will not develop as quickly as their oral and aural skills. This can have implications for placing students in levels as they may be Level 3 in some areas but only Level 2 in others. Most institutions will have a policy to cope with this discrepancy and may require you to introduce remedial literacy work to enhance reading and writing skills.

Integrating skills

> *Many teachers take an integrated skills approach so that students have the opportunity to practise all four skills during the lesson, with the main focus on speaking.*

One way to integrate the skills is through setting tasks that learners have to complete cooperatively. Here is a definition of **task** from Jane Willis (1996: 23):

> *'Tasks are activities where the target language is used by the learner for a communicative purpose in order to achieve a goal.'*

Deciding ten things to take as a group to a desert island would be a task (there is a reason to speak and there is an outcome), whereas filling gaps with examples of a particular tense would not (the purpose of the activity is to practise grammar and not to communicate ideas).

An integrated skills task might involve learners gathering information from various reading texts (reading), discussing the information with their partners (listening and speaking) and producing a poster of the most important issues or points (writing). The teacher, acting as a resource, can work on grammar and vocabulary as it arises from the context, rather than deciding in advance what language the students will need. In other words, language work is also integrated.

The advantage of a task-based approach, apart from the skills practice, is that learners are involved at all stages in using the target language. If other students don't understand them, they must rethink and reformulate in order to get their meanings across. The focus is on successful communication, which is both rewarding and motivating, rather than on practice per se. It shows the building-bloc approach to language and has inherently motivating qualities through the sense of achievement on completion of tasks.

In the final lesson plan, we present a task-based learning activity, adapted from *Collins Cobuild Books,* that could be used with any language:

Lesson plan 5	*Name of tutor:* Monika Finnegan	*Class:* Level 2 German	*No. in group:* 15	*Date:* 10.10.03	*Time:* 9.30–11.30am

Aims:	to give students opportunities to use the language they have to communicate; to help students to pick out key vocabulary and phrases from an authentic listening activity; to focus on *werde* + verb as a way to express hypothetical meaning.

Topic	**New vocabulary**	**Phonology points**
• Restaurants and guests for dinner	• Types of restaurant	

Language work	**Skills work**	**Anticipated problems**
• *werde* + verb	• Listening to native speakers doing task and picking out key phrases	• Students might find the speakers on tape speak too quickly. The tapescript should help if this is the case

Time	**Teacher's activity**	**T< >S? S< >S?**	**Student's activity**	**Objective**	**Materials**
9.30	Welcome students and ask them what they had for dinner last night. Discuss favourite food.	T< >S	Discuss topic with teacher.	Warm students up. Provide opportunity for informal chatting.	None
9.40	Pre-task Show students pictures of different types of restaurants. Ask ss to discuss: 1 What kind of restaurants they are. 2 Which restaurant they would prefer to visit and why.	Groups	Answer questions.	Develop vocabulary for discussing food and restaurants. Personalise the topic by proffering opinion re food.	Pictures of different restaurants
9.55	Feedback	T< >S	Answer questions and offer opinions.	Opportunity to check what students know both in terms of vocabulary and in terms of target language.	See above
10.05	Set task. What would you cook for someone who dropped in unexpectedly for dinner? *Was würde man für einen unerwarteten Gast kochen?*	T< >S Groups	Students listen to task and then discuss their answers.	Focus on meaning – learners try to communicate their ideas with the language they have.	
10.20	Visit each group and appoint one secretary to make notes and report group's findings to the class.	T< >S Groups	Students work with the secretary to produce a written report of their ideas.	As students write, they focus on the accuracy of what they want to say.	None

Lesson plan 5	Name of tutor: Monika Finnegan	Class: Level 2 German		No. in group: 15	Date: 10.10.03	Time: 9.30–11.30am

Time	Teacher's activity	T< >S? S< >S?	Student's activity	Objective	Materials
10. 30	Report stage. Students read out reports.	Groups	Listen to ideas from other groups.	Students practise listening to each other and valuing what others say.	None
10.45	Input stage. Tell students they will hear a tape of native speakers doing the same task. They must listen and decide which person would prepare what dish. Play tape more than once if necessary.	S S< >S	Listen to tape and note answers. Discuss answers in pairs before feedback.	Listen to authentic language use. Students identify key language.	Tape
11.00	Feedback. Focus on language. Ask students what kind of words the native speakers used to express their ideas.	T< >S	Suggest answers.	Focus on new language.	Tape
11.15	Distribute tapescripts. Ask students to underline examples of *werde* +verb.				

Jane Willis in her book *A framework for task-based learning* lists and explains a number of different tasks for integrating skills in this way. Here is a list of task types taken from this book:

- **listing**: e.g. qualities, characteristics, job-related skills;
- **ordering and sorting**: e.g. jumbled lists, ranking, categorising, classifying;
- **comparing**: e.g. matching, finding similarities, finding differences;
- **problem solving**: e.g. logic problems, real life problems, incomplete stories, case studies;
- **sharing personal experiences**: e.g. anecdotes, personal reminiscences, attitudes and opinions, personal reactions;
- **creative tasks**: e.g. fact-finding, writing poems stories, producing magazine/webpage.

Language work

Language-learning lessons traditionally focused on the grammar and vocabulary of a language. All too often this prevails to this day. Clara, talking about her Japanese lesson, told us:

 Controlled practice activities of new grammar take up most of the lesson.

And Phoebe said of her Greek lesson:

> *We did a lot of vocabulary. We wrote down zillions of words and what they meant.*

Learners generally want to speak and write accurately and to be able to produce the correct word at the right time. What is more, they want language lessons that are motivating and useful. In the following sections we will discuss how we can bring these two elements together so that teaching and learning grammar and vocabulary is relevant, efficient and effective.

Teaching and learning grammar

Frances assures us that grammar work isn't necessarily unpopular:

> *There has always got to be a grammar element ... I want to get the grammar right.*

However, teachers of languages can face problems when dealing with grammar because of their learners' grammatical knowledge. When we asked a group of MFL teachers how they would describe their British students' grammatical knowledge, their feelings were summed up in the following response:

> *It is very poor! Most students don't understand grammar.*

Each teacher was also keen to point out that there were students who do not fit this profile and whose language awareness is strong. For many, however, poor grammatical understanding can be a barrier to learning the foreign language, especially when the technical side is emphasised in the classroom.

In the following section we will look at different ways of approaching grammar teaching which do not rely too much on technical knowledge or on teacher explanation. The focus is on getting learners to use and practise the new grammar quickly and efficiently and on getting students to **notice** features and paradigms of new grammatical items, which research suggests can lead to acquisition (Schmidt 1990). I will then suggest ways in which students can organise their vocabulary learning successfully.

Presentation approach: as the name suggests, this approach presents new grammar in an explicit way to the learners. Usually the target forms are put into a typical **context** of use for the learners and then the teacher draws attention to the **form, meaning and use** of the grammatical item. In the following example the language is Japanese, and the target forms are making comparisons:

Chang: This morning I came to work by train for the first time. It was awfully crowded. It was terrible.
Smith: Trains are faster than cars, though. Because the roads are crowded.
Chang: How do you come to the office everyday?
Smith: I come and go by subway. The subway is the most convenient of all transportation systems in Tokyo.

Chang: Is the subway crowded mornings and evenings?
Smith: Yes. The mornings are more crowded than the evenings, etc.

(Adapted from *Japanese for busy people*, Bk 2)

As you can see, there are plenty of examples of comparatives here. After learners have read through or listened to the dialogue, the teacher can use the examples of comparatives in the text to demonstrate the grammatical rules of the forms. Students can then practise the new forms by answering questions about, for example, the transport system in their own country.

Discovery methods: these are methods that encourage learners to look at language and make judgements about how the grammar works. Teachers ask questions rather than give explanations and guide the learners to make their own grammar rules. In the following description of a beginners' lesson in Italian, Liz explains how she has used this method successfully:

I wanted to try an inductive approach to teaching this grammar point. In the past, I have taught it by giving examples of words students know in the singular and then in the plural, for example:

un libro	*libri*
una finestra	*due finestre*
un bicchiere	*due biccieri*
una televisione	*due televisioni*

I then wrote up the patterns on the board:

> *-o- -i-*
> *-a- -e-*
> *-e- -i-*

But as this is difficult for English speakers of Italian to remember, I felt that introducing this point inductively would help learners remember the rule. I gave students in groups of three the following handout:

Look at these words:

panini birre libri cappuccini finestre vini bicchieri vacanze macchine gelati porte studenti televisioni penne matite

a. How do we make nouns plural in Italian?

b. How do we make the plural on femine nouns ending in 'a'?

c. How do we make the plural of masculine nounds ending in 'o'?

d. How do we make the plural of masc/fem nouns ending in 'e'?

I asked the students what they thought of the exercise. They were enthusiastic and said they thought working out the rule together helped them to remember it better.

Discovery approaches can be particularly useful for native teachers of a language who have not studied their own language formally or who cannot explain in the students' first language. Frances describes how her teacher gets round this problem:

The teacher herself will say, 'I don't know how to explain it but I know how to explain it by example'.

A discovery approach, then, for both teachers and learners.

Chunking: this approach relies less on grammar as the organising principle of language and more on vocabulary. Teachers encourage learners to record and learn fixed and semi-fixed phrases rather than individual words to which they have to apply grammar rules. For example, in English, learners can be taught the phrase, ***Could you pass the* _____ , *please?*** which can generate an infinite number of requests. This might prove more useful in the long term than spending a lesson focusing on when to use 'a' and when 'the', or on giving an overview of the modal 'could'.

There are a number of benefits of this approach:

- learners feel that they are progressing quickly in the language;
- there is a focus on pronunciation in phrasing rather than individual words, making speaking and listening easier;
- learners can begin to generalise rules about grammar from the phrases they are learning rather than trying to make phrases from the grammar they are learning.

Phoebe was sympathetic to this approach:

I would have preferred to learn more useful phrases and sentences and then I think they might have become more apparent to me. I might have been able to transfer grammatical structures from one context to another.

You can use this technique immediately in the classroom without much deviating from what you do normally. Rather than writing up individual words on the board, show how these words are commonly used in phrases, indicating which elements can be changed:

Yaya | *lafiya?*
      | *iyali?*
      | *aiki?*

In the Hausa example given above, the phrase 'Yaya' (meaning 'how ...?') can be followed by any number of noun phrases (here: how are you? how is your home? how is your work?). Students can learn this pattern without worrying about the grammatical relationship *'yaya'* has with other clause elements.

Rehearsal: recent research is showing that learners who are given the opportunity to repeat tasks and activities use language in a more complex and accurate way in repetitions (Bygate). Planning time also seems to have benefits for both accuracy and complexity. Again, this is a simple change to make to classroom procedure and one that mirrors authentic and likely communicative challenges in the target language country: give learners a few minutes before a speaking or writing activity to plan what they want to say. Be available in this time so that you can respond to individual learners' questions. After the activity provide feedback on problems and useful language that emerged, and then let the learners have another go, perhaps with a different partner.

Clara's teacher of Japanese mainly uses a presentation approach. Learners are given plenty of opportunity to listen to and practise new forms, but Clara does not think this is enough:

Neither the textbook nor the teacher give much in the way of explanations about grammar. I am quite interested in the mechanics. I think we should have the chance to talk about the language as well as the opportunity to use it.

Introducing a 'grammar surgery' each month or term is one way of addressing learners' individual grammar needs. Learners can nominate grammatical topics to be covered in advance to give you time to research the answers and find ways to explain them. A similar scheme has recently been introduced in the Languages and European Studies Department at Aston University as a direct response to undergraduate learners' individual problems with grammar.

Teaching and learning vocabulary

Many students rank knowing vocabulary above grammar when they talk about what is important when learning a foreign language. Before we can discuss how vocabulary is best acquired, let's look at what we mean by knowing a word.

Knowing a word

What is involved in knowing a word? Meaning is extremely important, but when a word has more than one meaning, students should at least know the **core meaning.** This is the definition a native speaker would give if asked for one. They also need to know:

■ the orthographical form of the word;
■ how to pronounce it;
■ how it behaves grammatically;
■ its collocations (what words frequently occur with it);
■ how frequent it is;
■ what registers it occurs in (is it formal or informal, for example).

It is unlikely that a student will learn all these things at the same time. It is more likely that information about the word will be learnt little by little and that a learner's knowledge of a word will develop over time. This has a number of implications for teaching:

■ students should be given opportunities to practise using the word;
■ students should record vocabulary systematically;
■ students should revise vocabulary regularly.

Practising vocabulary

Frances told us:

When I learn a new word, I try to get it into conversation as soon as I can.

Phoebe also said she liked to use the words or phrases as much as possible after she had learnt them:

When I was driving along, for example, when I'd just learnt directions, I drove my family mad by saying straight ahead all the time, and turn right.

This demonstrates the importance of learner initiative in terms of practising new words and phrases. In the same way that we might try to use a person's name soon after being introduced to him/her so as not to forget it, learners need to be aware that consciously using the word themselves can aid retention.

Teachers can of course introduce many kinds of activities to the class to practise vocabulary:

- 'pictionary' (a student draws a word and the other students guess which word it is);
- 'taboo' (a students gives definitions or examples of a word and other students must guess which word is being described);
- categories (students have ten words from one category on a card and students have to call out as many items as they can remember from that category. If they are on the card, they are crossed off);
- word stories (students choose a number of words from a list and write a story which includes these words).

You can find a number of really useful and entertaining activities for practising vocabulary in *Pair work*, by Peter Watcyn-Jones, and in Classic Pathfinder 4: *Doing it for themselves* by Vee Harris and David Snow.

Recording vocabulary

There is no doubt that **memorisation** is a key feature in learning vocabulary. In order to make memorisation easier, learners need to record vocabulary in an organised way. This can be done by exploiting relationships between words, which also links to what we know about how our brains retain words.

Our learners need to keep vocabulary records, usually in the form of a vocabulary notebook. There are various ways that learners can then record their vocabulary.

Traditionally, learners recorded a word with a translation as the word came up in class or in their reading. The vocabulary entry for Cantonese would look something like this:

> *fahn* = rice
> *yingwokyahn* = English person
> *nido* = here

There is some merit in this approach. The word is recorded; the meaning is clear and the list approach makes it easy to sit and learn for short periods of time. There may well be value too in the fact that the words bear little relationship to each other; at least this way they are not confused. Nevertheless, even a list approach such as this could be more informative. For example, the word class could be given (adjective? verb? phrase?) and in the case of tonal languages such as Cantonese, information about tone could be added (high falling etc). There could be a note about register (formal? informal? neutral?) and how the word is used in a phrase (*'Nido m'goi.'* Drop me here, please).

Another approach would be to record the words in families. Part of the notebook could be set aside for this purpose. For example, here is an entry for furniture vocabulary in an French learner's notebook:

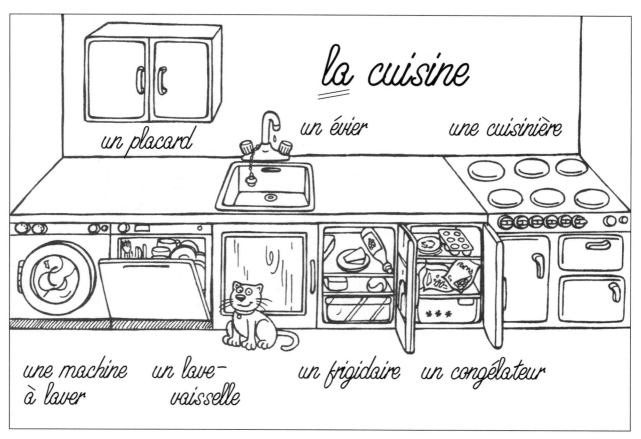

la cuisine

un placard — un évier — une cuisinière

une machine à laver — un lave-vaisselle — un frigidaire — un congélateur

un canapé — un halogène

une table de salon

un fauteuil

une télévision*

le salon

le rideau de douche

le lavabo

la douche

la baignoire (je l'adore!)

la descente de bain

les toilettes

* un lecteur DVD, un magnétoscope, une chaîne hifi.

En France, en général, les toilettes ne sont pas dans la salle de bains.

NB: les toilettes

la toilette

The student has grouped items found in the same room together, has given information about word class and has provided quick sketches of items to help her to remember the item.

Another section of the notebook could be given over to idioms in the target language. In English, for example, the verb 'get' forms collocations with lots of other words to produce idiomatic phrases:

GET	
get + noun	**get + prepositional phrase**
get a life	get on with someone
get a job	get out

In our classes we are likely to observe a variety of strategies employed by our learners for recording vocabulary, and therefore varying levels of support are needed. Some learners may benefit from making an audio recording of new vocabulary, others may find it easier to remember vocabulary they recorded on a visually enhanced presentation software, such as Microsoft PowerPoint.

Revising vocabulary

Once the vocabulary has been recorded, students have to learn it. Little and often probably works best. Here are some ideas that students have told us about for learning vocabulary:

- write names of items around the house on sticky labels and stick them on the matching item;
- each time you meet a new word, write it on a small piece of paper with the definition or translation on the back. Put all the pieces into a bag. Each day, pull out ten pieces of paper. Look at the word; if you can provide the definition, then throw it away. If you can't remember what it means, put it back in the bag;
- each time you meet a new word, write it on a card with word information. File the word. Every day, take eight to ten words out of the file and put them in your pocket. Look at the words at least six times during the day. If at the end of the day you know the word, throw it away. If you don't, re-file it;
- when you look up a word in a dictionary, mark the word with a green spot. If you have to look up the word again, mark it with a blue spot. If you have to look it up for the third time, you know it is an important word that you can't remember! Mark it with a red spot and write it into your vocabulary note book.

Features of successful teaching and learning

Autonomy is a crucial element in helping our learners to be successful.

Earlier I said that success in the classroom depends to a large extent on how we teach and what we teach. In the first part of this section I will explore the teacher's role in successful teacher-learner interaction, drawing on years of practice as a language teacher and countless observations of other teachers' lessons as a teacher trainer. In the second part I will look more closely at the learners. Unless our learners are motivated to learn, what we teach and how we teach it will have little impact. We need to harness and develop autonomous learning in our students.

The teacher's role

When we asked Frances, who is a hardworking, diligent and ambitious student, for the qualities of a successful foreign language teacher, she answered:

> *You've got to be open and likeable and a good communicator ... you have to be articulate ... and a bit gregarious ... you know, anecdotal ... and creative.*

Later on she justified her opinion by saying:

> *With a language, communication is half the battle.*

Phoebe, too, felt that personal qualities are more important than teaching skills:

> *They need to be able to enthuse you.*

As did Clara:

> *A key quality is that they are enthusiastic about their subject and that they can bring their learners with them.*

It is both encouraging and worrying that these three learners rank personality above skill: encouraging in that it suggests that teachers do not necessarily need experience and training to succeed as teachers; worrying in that it is difficult to acquire such personal qualities if you do not naturally have them, not to mention the inherent difficulties with all aspects of a departmental framework for teacher support and continuing professional development.

During the interview, Frances and Phoebe did highlight teaching skills that teachers should have, such as giving examples of grammar, being able to explain the host culture and being competent users of the language. Phoebe and Clara also highlighted the role of the teacher as 'structurer' of the lesson. However, it is obviously central that teachers have strong interpersonal skills and that learners are valued as people, not just students.

> *The good language teacher values the individual student in the classroom.*

While it is gratifying that learners can be forgiving of teachers, teacher trainers tend to be less so! Nevertheless, the following list of qualities of a good language teacher devised by Jim Scrivener also features a number of personal characteristics. He believes the effective teacher:

- really listens to students;
- shows respect;
- gives clear, positive feedback;
- has a good sense of humour;
- is patient;
- knows the subject;
- inspires confidence;
- trusts people;
- empathises with students' problems;
- is well-organised;
- paces lessons well;
- does not complicate things unnecessarily;
- is enthusiastic and inspires enthusiasm;

- can be authoritative without being distant;
- is honest;
- is approachable.

Accommodating the individual language learner

The first two characteristics on Scrivener's list – *really listens to students and shows respect* – demonstrate that the good language teacher values the individual student in the classroom. Other ways the teacher can do this are to accommodate both learners' preferred learning styles and their learning abilities. We will now look at how these two aims can be achieved.

Accommodating learner styles

> **Learners prefer to learn different things and in different ways.**

In order to accommodate learners' preferences in a class, we have to provide a **variety** of activities. Phoebe became quite frustrated when the teacher always followed the same procedures:

> *The teacher would do most of the talking and when we needed to practise something she would go round the whole group one person at a time. If there was a dialogue she would take one part and the students would take another part ... the whole thing would take about twenty minutes and you would only get your three minutes of glory. I found that quite boring.*

Clara, too, cited lack of variety as a reason why she did not learn as much as she could:

> *The lack of variety doesn't help. I find that quite a barrier, the fact that the class always starts in the same way means I switch off mentally – oh no, not that again. Generally I am someone who needs a lot of variety.*

In terms of classroom procedures, here are some suggestions:

- aim for a balance between activities that focus on language description (for analytical learners) and activities that focus on language use (for holistic learners);
- allow students to talk to each other in pairs and groups. This will go some way to providing the kind of support holistic students need;
- set work that enables students to discover rules about how language works to accommodate analytical learners;
- provide both visual and auditory support when introducing new language: if the new language is first modelled orally, at some point provide a written version, and vice versa;
- introduce activities that encourage movement. Information gathering from sites around the room, for example, provides a clear skills focus at the same time as accommodating kinesthetic learning;
- take the learners out of the classroom. Frances told us that the most enjoyable aspect of her Hebrew learning experience was being invited to her teacher's house for dinner. Here the culture had come alive, the conversation had been natural, with learners being given the opportunity to use the language over a period of time;
- use ICT appropriately for authentic stimulus as well as to provide an additional tool for kinesthetic learners who might benefit form the physical and dynamic involvement with language through another medium.

Accommodating learners' abilities

Just as students have different approaches to learning a language and different purposes to their learning, so they will have different strengths and weaknesses in their linguistic abilities. Some may be strong orally but struggle with reading or writing, while others may find it difficult to use grammar accurately but have good listening skills. Teachers will need to use **differentiation strategies** in order to keep learners with such different abilities focused on learning throughout the lesson.

In their excellent book ResourceFile 4: *Mixed-ability teaching in language learning,* Susan Ainslie and Susan Purcell suggest a number of useful strategies for coping with differentiation. In terms of planning they suggest that learning objectives for each lesson should be differentiated as follows:

- **core** aims should be achieved by all students;
- **reinforcement** aims push more able students to achieve more;
- **extension** aims provide a good level of challenge for those whose understanding or capability exceeds others in the class.

Developing class aims from this perspective can help the teacher to keep all students motivated and learning.

Grouping and pairing students can help or exacerbate the challenges of mixed-ability teaching. Teachers must consider if grouping weak students together and strong students together will result in the most productive learning environment. Weaker students often enjoy the help, support and understanding that stronger students can provide, while strong students can enjoy guiding those who need their help. Watching closely while students work together can help teachers decide on successful groupings and pairings for all students in the class.

Further strategies for accommodating social, affective and intellectual differences in the classroom can be found in Pathfinder 37: *Differentiation and individual learners* by Ann Convery and Do Coyle.

The successful language learner

There has been a good deal of research into characteristics and motivations of adult language learners, some of which have been discussed in Chapter 2. The characteristic that all the researchers believe good language learners share, however, is the ability to study the language outside the classroom, be this formally or informally. Julian Edge emphasises this point when he discusses the teacher's role:

> *'So, can we say that the teacher must organise, provide security, motivate, instruct, model, guide, inform, give feedback, encourage and evaluate? Yes, but the best teachers do something else, too. In a way that suits the individuals, society and culture concerned, they encourage learners to take on some responsibility in these areas.'*

Students unused to studying a language may need support and guidance in developing autonomous learning skills. In the following sections I suggest what kind of guidance and help to give in order to better equip students with the necessary skills and confidence.

Autonomous learning in the classroom

Students can provide material for the classroom by bringing in language-learning resources, such as newspaper articles, brochures or words and expressions they have picked up on the radio or Internet. You can then use these as teaching materials or you can ask students to prepare questions or presentations based on the materials. If you are teaching a language for which there are few published resources available, such practical help can be invaluable.

Individual learning plans

Many adult learner institutions are beginning to collect Individual Learning Plans (ILP) from their students. This document is completed by the student and the teacher together and is a statement of what the student will achieve during the term and how he/she will cover it. The ILP covers not only classwork but also the work that the learner will do independently, recognising the value of student autonomy. Long-term and short-term goals are set, as are timescales for goal completion. Page 88 shows an ILP developed by the English Department at Brasshouse Language Centre.

In order for the ILP to be successful, it needs to be taken seriously by the institution, teacher and learner. The **institution** can demonstrate its commitment by dedicating time to ILP completion in the timetable. It should not be a document that is completed in a hurry or in place of learning but rather should have its role within the negotiated learning process. Learners should also be made aware of the ILP when they register for a course and be given written guidance about its role in the overall teaching approach and how it supports the individual learner in achieving his or her individual learning outcomes.

The **teacher** needs to consider carefully how the learner's goals are to be achieved. While it is tempting to transfer information from the scheme of work directly on to the ILP document, this will not meet individual learner's needs in all cases. Think about texts the learners can access, audio and visual tapes they can play and remedial language work they can address and how they can do this. Be realistic with what each learner can achieve in the time they have available for private study.

Learners have to believe the ILP is a valuable document that requires a commitment from them. They should know how much time per week they can dedicate to studying, what areas they wish to improve and what approaches they prefer when studying.

The Council of Europe's **European Language Portfolio** (ELP) also supports individual language learning by encouraging learners to reflect on and improve their language learning, whether a student is learning in class or individually. It also acts as a record of achievement in language learning and in cultural awareness which is recognised throughout Europe. An additional advantage of the ELP is that it is applicable to any language. Given the lack of accreditation opportunities, for example for community languages, the ELP might have a place particularly for recording achievement in high-level community language learning.

A progress charting document such as the ELP also supports efforts around departmental or institutional quality assurance and standardisation since it is based on the National Language Standards (NLS) and the Common European Framework. CILT have produced two versions of this document, one for young language learners (primary sector) and one for adults (see Appendix, p132).

Brasshouse Language Centre   **Individual Learning Plan 2004– 2005**

Name: _____   Date: _____   Learner ID: _____

Centre assessment

First language:

Other languages:

Initial assessment made by:

Previous learning experience, including exams taken:

Placement test score:

Summmary of assessment:

Your goals

What made you decide to enrol on a course at Brasshouse (work related, to get a qualification, personal development)?

What do you want to be able to use your English for in one year's time?

What do you want to be able to use your English for in three year's time?

Do you have a target goal (e.g. IELTS score, Cambridge Examination, TOEFL score)?

Your course at Brasshouse

The course/courses you will take are:

The number of guided learning hours are:

The course will help you specifically to:

We will measure improvement by:

Learning outside the class

Outside class the number of hours you will study per week will be: _____

This means you will study altogether for _____ hours over the term.

You will focus particularly on improving the following:

You will measure improvement by:

Other things you can do to develop your language skills (e.g. joining clubs, finding work, etc):

Reviewing progress

You will discuss your progress with your tutor on:

Before the meeting, your tutor will gather the following information and evidence concerning your progress:

Before the meeting, you will gather the following information and evidence concerning your progress:

Signed (student)

Signed (tutor)

Information and Communication Technologies (ICT)

Without wanting to evoke a much over-used cliché, it has to be said that the pace of technological development and fast increasing user skills have changed teaching and learning opportunities, as well as learners' expectations in and outside the language classroom. Although the reality in many institutions in terms of ICT equipment and training is often far removed from the perceived ideal, good practice is evolving and can be observed in many classrooms. The range of ICT equipment integrated into language teaching and learning varies from the tried and tested audio technology, through CD-ROMs, the Internet and other software applications such as PowerPoint, Word, Hot Potatoes, to high-tech classrooms with interactive whiteboards and wireless laptop technology.

While it would be beyond the framework of a book such as this to investigate in detail the different types of ICT, I would like to refer here to some strategies for the exploitation of the Internet in the context of language learning and teaching (see also the reference section of this chapter with pointers to some books on this topic; it is also worth following postings and publications on sites such as BECTA, Nesta and CILT).

Frances told us that she relies on the Internet for language practice outside the classroom:

> *I try to read Hebrew newspapers on the Internet every week.*

Clara uses the 'teach yourself Japanese' sites to practise reading *kana* and *kanji*. Certainly, encouraging learners to access sites as part of a self-study programme of learning is one way of exploiting the huge amount of language learning material that now exists on the Internet. But there are other ways. In order to discuss these, I have divided the following Internet information into three areas:

1 dedicated teaching sites;
2 dedicated language-learning sites;
3 general sites.

We will explore the benefits of each in turn.

Dedicated teaching sites

There are a number of sites which provide materials and activities for teaching modern foreign languages. These sites may also suggest useful resources and teaching associations (see Appendix, p132).

Dedicated learning sites

Finding sites that learners can access in order to study independently gives teachers an extra option when setting homework (for a fuller discussion of homework, see the section below). Teachers can also download activities from these sites for use in the classroom and students can work through the exercises at their own pace.

There are a number of sites on the Internet that require payment before access is permitted: a number of other sites survive by advertising other products on their site. Before recommending any sites, including those listed in the Appendix (p133), visit the site and explore it thoroughly. Like course books, websites can promise more than they deliver!

The Internet in particular has changed how learners are able to access up-to-date and authentic resources either in the classroom or independently.

General sites

The vast majority of information on the web has not been designed for teaching languages. However, it does represent a huge resource which can be used by teachers and learners for this purpose. For many teachers living and working in the UK, it provides the best source of authentic and up-to-date material for the classroom, supplementing and sometimes replacing coursebook material. As with all authentic material, however, teachers need to select material which interests learners and which learners can understand, at least to some extent.

When selecting material from the Web, consider the following:

- is the subject matter interesting for the students?
- do students need to have a specialised knowledge to understand the texts?
- do the texts have a high level of idiomatic (colloquial) language and, if so, do students have a good command of idiomatic language?
- is the text supported by visual information such as diagrams and photographs?
- what do you want students to do with the text? Do they have to understand every word or is a basic understanding of gist enough?
- can you explain to students the purpose of reading the text?

Here are a number of approaches for teaching using the Internet. Many more ideas can be found in InfoTech 7: *Communicating on-line* by Sabine Gläsmann, InfoTech 3: *WWW/The Internet in the modern foreign languages classroom* by Terry Atkinson, and *How to use the Internet in ELT* by Teeler and Gray.

➤ ➤ Teaching and practising structures and vocabulary

You can use texts found on the Internet in the same way as coursebook material to teach new structures and vocabulary. Clive Newson, of Liverpool University, suggests using the information that search engines provide for this purpose. For example, you can ask students to research the weather in different cities for the next few days around the world. Students then exchange the information practising future forms and weather vocabulary (e.g. *Il fait beau aujourd'hui à Paris mais* demain *il va faire mauvais*), perhaps using a table such as this:

	Tokyo	Rio	Jakarta	Moscow
Aujourd'hui	il fait beau			
Demain	il va pleuvoir			

➤ ➤ Webquests

A Webquest is an 'inquiry –oriented activity in which some or all of the information that learners interact with comes from resources on the Internet' (Dodge). Webquests offer a structured approach to information gathering as students use the information that they find to complete a task, often replicating real workplace tasks. There are four phases to each webquest:

- Introduction
- Task
- Process
- Evaluation

Students work independently and the role of the teacher is to offer guidance when needed.

To find out more about webquests, visit the sites listed in the Appendix (p133).

➤ ➤ Penpals

Communicating with penpals or keypals is a fast, authentic and motivating approach to writing in the target language. Messages can be written in class or as homework and can be checked by the teacher before being sent. Once initial contact and introductions have been made, topics can be set for each e-mail – for example, my hometown, my family, summer festivals, learning a language – so that students have a reason to write.

Finding keypals is obviously the first step in this process. If your students are English speakers, you should be able to pair them up with students from the target culture quite easily as there are huge numbers of students throughout the world learning English. Students can take it in turns to write in the language they are learning and they have the benefit of reading texts written by an expert user. Another approach is to find students who are studying the same language as your learners. Institutions similar to the one you are working in may have students interested in joining a keypal project.

If you have problems finding keypals, the website listed in the Appendix (p134) has pals in a number of countries looking for partners.

➤ ➤ Homework

Finally (and somewhat ironically?) a word on homework. All our learners said they valued this, and Phoebe made a particularly astute comment:

 The teacher gave us homework every week and she treated it quite seriously. She seemed to give it due seriousness. She always marked it and gave it back with comments on it and it was useful and it was good and if she hadn't given it to us I wouldn't have looked at the book from one week to the next.

In a Spanish class I attended recently, I was very impressed with the amount of homework the students produced and the care that had gone into producing it. Here are some ideas to help you make homework an essential element of the learning experience:

■ plan what homework you will give and write this into your scheme of work;

■ focus on the homework during the lesson, not at the end when students are keen to go home and are already focused on other things. Write the homework on the board and ensure all learners have noted it down;

■ collect the homework each lesson. Make time for this, perhaps half way through the lesson when all the students have arrived. If a student hasn't completed the homework, speak to him/her about it (perhaps in the coffee break or after class);

■ mark the homework and give it back as quickly as possible;

■ respond to content as well as accuracy when you mark;

■ develop a code for marking homework so that it takes you less time and so that learners can correct it themselves: _ can mean 'word missing', for example;

■ think about using an e-mail system for submitting work. You can mark it on-line and send it back very quickly;

■ if you want to go over homework in class, give yourself a time limit. Make sure checking the homework takes up no more than 25% of class time.

Remember that the teacher needs to value homework if students are to value it too.

Conclusion

What I have presented here are some thoughts and ideas about how teaching and learning foreign languages can be managed in the classroom. It is not meant to be a definitive guide and nor would I suggest that these approaches will work for everyone in every context. Rather, they are ideas and approaches that have worked for us or for teachers we know.

Earlier in the chapter I mentioned the reflective practitioner, the teacher who looks at teaching and learning as an experience that can be continually analysed and developed. I would like to end this chapter by asking you to become reflective practitioners by trying out the ideas presented here, but then to take time to reflect on what aspects worked, which did not and for what reasons. Taking this approach will help you to develop into the best teacher that you can be, and a valued member of the professional community of foreign language teachers.

References

Ainslie, S. and Purcell, S. (2001) ResourceFile4: *Mixed-ability teaching in language learning*. CILT.

Atkinson, T. (2002) InfoTech 3: WWW/*The Internet in the modern foreign languages classroom*. 2nd edition. CILT.

Bygate, M. (2001) 'Effects of task repetition on the structure and control of oral language'. In Bygate, M., Skehan, P. and Swain, M. *Researching pedagogic tasks, second language learning, teaching and testing*. Longman.

Convery, A. and Coyle, D. (1999) Pathfinder 37: *Differentiation and individual learners: a guide for classroom practice*. CILT.

Dodge, B. (1995) *Some thoughts about webquests*. http://edweb.sdsu.edu/courses/edtec596/about_webquests.html

Edge, J. (1998) *The essentials of English language teaching*. Longman.

Ellis, R. (1990) *Instructed second language acquisition*. Blackwell.

Gläsmann, S. (2003) InfoTech 7: *Communicating on-line*. CILT.

Harris, V. and Snow, D. (2004) Classic Pathfinder 4: *Doing it for themselves. Focus on learning strategies and vocabulary building*. CILT.

Krashen, S. (1985) *The input hypothesis*. Longman.

Languages National Training Organisation (2000) *The National Language Standards 2000*.

Nuttall, C. (2000) *Teaching reading skills in a foreign language*. Macmillan Heinemann.

Schmidt, R. (1990) 'The role of consciousness in second language learning'. *Applied Linguistics*, 11: 17–46.

Scrivener, J. (1994) *Learning teaching*. Macmillan Heinemann.

Teeler, D. and Gray, P. (2000) *How to use the Internet in ELT*. Longman.

Ur, P. (1981) *Discussions that work*. Cambridge University Press.

Watcyn-Jones, P. (1997) *Pair work*. Penguin.

Willis, J. (1996) *A framework for task based learning*. Longman.

Willis, J. and Willis, D. (1988) *Cobuild Books*. Collins.

White, R. and Arndt, V. (1991) *Process writing*. Longman.

5 Measuring learning

■ Susan Ainslie

'I don't want to spend my time assessing; I want to teach.'
(Adult education teacher, Cheshire, May 2002)

This chapter attempts to clarify what we mean by measuring learning and discusses a range of strategies for integrating it into the cycle of teaching and learning without detracting from the quality of the learning experiencee, but rather enhancing it.

Measuring learning encompasses the notion of assessment, which tutors are often reluctant to get involved in, fearing that it could demotivate learners by highlighting their inadequacies and detract from the enjoyment of the learning experience. Tutors are keen to teach in as imaginative, interesting and varied a way as they can, so that learners are enthused by the subject and keen to continue to learn. Learners may also not want to be involved in being tested; they report that they are attending an adult education class for enjoyment, or to pick up some language to enable them to communicate while on holiday, and not because they are seeking a qualification.

> **Measuring learning does not need to be a negative experience.**

Measuring learning is achieved in a variety of ways, of which formal testing is only one. Carefully planned and integrated into our teaching, it can improve the quality of the learning experience for our learners. It enables the tutor and the learner to identify strengths and areas for development on a group and an individual basis, and this can inform subsequent lesson planning.

The range of ways in which learning can be measured is very wide and the decisions that the tutor makes about how to assess learning will depend on a number of factors. Whatever the nature of our course, however, we need to know what our learners have learnt. The teacher quoted above, whose comment is echoed by many others, probably incorporates strategies into her lessons to check that the learners can demonstrate achievement of her learning objectives. She will probably also use what she knows to inform her future planning.

Adult education courses may be accredited or non-accredited. While tutors on accredited courses recognise that they have to ensure that they are preparing for the requirements of a specific examining board, non-accredited classes must also have learning objectives that the teacher hopes will be achieved, and it is important to measure learning systematically against these objectives. At the time of writing a national recognition scheme, the 'Languages Ladder', is about to be launched (see Appendix, p134, for more details).

What do we mean by measuring learning?

Learning can be measured in a **formal** way – by tests or examinations set by an external accrediting or examining body so that the results can be compared regionally, nationally or internationally, or by tests devised by the institution or the authority for which we work to compare across teaching groups, or by the individual tutor. Tests devised by the individual teacher can be targeted at the specific learning objectives of our courses, whereas those set by other bodies cannot take account of the content or context of one specific course. Nevertheless, accrediting bodies do provide detailed information about their requirements and course tutors or managers select accrediting bodies to match as closely as possible their learners' perceived needs, and tutors can therefore plan their courses to prepare their learners for forthcoming examinations or tests. Formal assessment usually measures learning at the end of a course, although some accrediting bodies measure a **portfolio of evidence** or **coursework** compiled by the learner under the guidance of the tutor during the course, a form of **continuous assessment**. Assessment may include both end of course and continuous assessment. Formal tests will normally have marking schemes and clear assessment criteria; these should be shared with the learners.

What is learning measured against?

It can be against regional, national or international standards, against other learners in a class, or against oneself, i.e. how much progress have I made? Have I understood what the teacher taught? It can be **criterion-referenced**, i.e. this is the standard, can I do it or not? Most examinations are criterion-referenced. Or it can be **norm-referenced**, i.e. how do I compare with the rest of the class? Theoretically, therefore, everyone in a class can 'pass' a criterion-referenced test, but a norm-referenced test enables only a percentage to succeed.

Learning can also be measured in an **informal** way. This is **monitoring,** an essential part of the teaching/learning process in order to check at each stage that learning has taken place. It includes:

- oral question and answer at the beginning of a lesson to check how much has been recalled from the previous lesson;
- tasks/exercises/activities which require learners to demonstrate comprehension – these should normally occur at several points during a lesson;
- the tutor moving round a class, listening to learners practising an oral activity or looking at written tasks, checking the progress that learners are making;
- marking classwork or 'homework' and giving feedback which includes setting targets for future development.

It is essential that these steps are incorporated into lesson planning, as the tutor cannot otherwise be sure that what he or she is teaching is being learnt. In plenary question/answer sessions tutors must also be cognisant of the learners who are not volunteering to answer – is this because they do not feel comfortable with answering in front of the rest of the group, even though they understand the objectives of the lesson, or is it because they have not understood? So monitoring must consider the individual as well as the group.

We measure learning for different purposes at different stages in the learning process. The measure may be:

- **diagnostic** – to identify strengths and weaknesses and plan accordingly, often at the beginning of a course;
- **formative** – measuring progress during a course and taking remedial action when necessary; or
- **summative** – measuring overall achievement at the end of a course.

> *Learning is measured effectively when the learner is involved in the process of identifying strengths, weaknesses and areas for further study.*

The process of **self-assessment** helps the learner to become independent and autonomous. Self-assessment can also be followed by **iterative assessment**, which simply means that a test which has been taken once is taken again at a later stage. This can be very motivating as almost invariably the learner does much better the second time, and this provides clear and unequivocal proof of the learning that has taken place, learning of which the learner may not have been aware. Assessment may be undertaken by the class tutor, by another teacher at the same institution, or by external examiners with no knowledge of the learner or the learning context. The assessor should be determined according to the purpose of the assessment.

Why measure learning?

The measurement of learning is part of an on-going cycle that involves the learner, the teacher, course organisers and external assessors. It has four key purposes:

1 to **monitor** the progress of individuals and groups on a course and identify areas for development;
2 to provide **guidance and feedback** to learners, individually and collectively;
3 to **test** achievement, perhaps also providing qualifications or certificates;
4 to help teachers, course organisers and external assessors to **evaluate** the effectiveness of courses.

For the tutor the cycle may be presented in the following way:

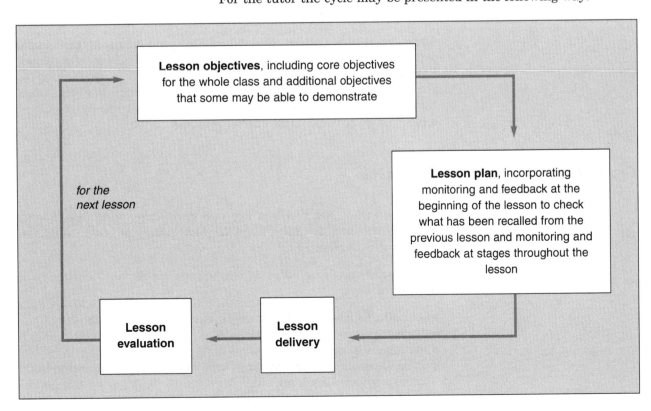

The following table expands on the above:

Stage	Includes	Questions for the tutor
Lesson objectives	Core objectives for everyone. Differentiated objectives for different members of the group.	What do I want the learners to be able to do at the end of the lesson? Which skills will this involve? What do I want everyone to be able to achieve and what do I want some learners to be able to achieve in addition?
Lesson plan and delivery	Recall at beginning of lesson. Monitoring and checking after each stage of the lesson. Recap at end to check that objectives have been met.	Do I need to go over aspects of the last lesson again? Which of the activities in my lesson will provide evidence of the learning that has taken place? How am I going to help individuals who may be struggling, without making them feel inadequate, while at the same time stretching learners who have been quick to grasp the new work?
Lesson evaluation	After the lesson, an evaluation of the teaching, and not just of the learning that has taken place – a key part of continuous improvement for the tutor.	Did everyone achieve the objectives I had set out before the lesson? If the learners did not seem to grasp what I was teaching, why was this? Was it too difficult, not clearly presented, too much at one time? How would I teach this differently next time?
Lesson objectives for the next lesson	Modified according to the previous lesson.	Do I need to go over some aspects of the last lesson? Do I need to build in additional activities for some of the learners, either to help them to consolidate the core objectives of the previous lesson, or to enable them to progress further/meet their individual objectives?

Added to this are more formal tests at appropriate stages in the learning process, at the end of a unit of work or at the end of a course. Language learning is a cumulative process, and learners need to remember what they did at the beginning of the course as well as what they did last week. Tests which include a review of earlier elements of a course help to consolidate overall progress.

From the learner's perspective

It is important that teachers exercise great care when planning to measure learning, because it can be very beneficial but can also be detrimental and damaging.

It can enhance the quality of the experience for the learner in a number of ways:

- it indicates how well they have mastered a particular topic;
- it gives pointers for future focus;
- it diagnoses strengths and areas for development;
- it builds confidence by showing them what they can do, and thereby gives a sense of achievement;

- it helps learners to develop their skills of self-assessment and therefore their autonomy;
- it helps learners to make realistic choices about future courses;
- research has demonstrated that the most important factor contributing to language-learning success is motivation. Most adult learners who come to a class are well-motivated to attend, though for a variety of reasons. A sense of progress and achievement through the measurement of learning will harness and strengthen the learner's motivation.

The measurement of learning can, however, have exactly the opposite effect:

- if it is pitched at too high a level, it can maker learners feel inadequate, by demonstrating to them what they cannot do, the progress they haven't made. It can make them feel that they are incapable of learning – older learners often fear that they are too old to learn;
- formal measurement of learning can create a sense of anxiety in learners, recalling the negative experiences they had of tests and examinations at school;
- all groups will have learners who are at different levels, which tutors generally try not to draw attention to in the group, but this is difficult to hide in the context of an assessment;
- there is a danger that lessons will focus on preparing learners for assessment, rather than on achieving appropriate learning goals;
- it can take up too great a proportion of lesson time, so that learners feel that they do not have enough time to progress in the language because there is too much assessment.

These factors can be hugely demotivating. A number of strategies can, however, be applied in order to avoid the potentially damaging effects on learners identified above.

1   The way the tutor approaches measuring and assessing learning is very important. It is essential to put learners at their ease and to reassure them from the outset that the courses will not involve a lot of 'testing' but rather that they will be doing activities that will help them and the teacher to appreciate the progress they are making, identify their strengths and areas for further development, and consequently to plan the course to meet their needs. The language teachers use is important – *I'd like you to try this activity and see how you get on* is much less threatening than *Next week I'm going to give you a test. I think it would be a good idea if you had another look at ...* is better than *You only got 6 out of 10*. A quiet word outside the class will be more helpful than discussing individual's difficulties in front of the rest of the class. Review the language used in the forms your learners need to complete: 'targets' or 'goals' may be better understood if instead you use phrases such as: *Things I still need to practise, I don't understand at all ...*

It is important to get to know your learners as well as possible as soon as possible.

2   A key to effective measurement of learning is to know your learners, as individuals and not just as a group, and to get to know them as early in the course as possible. We are much less likely to pitch an assessment activity at too high a level if we know well our learners' strengths and areas in need of further development. Decisions about lesson planning and its associated assessment must take into account our individual learners so that courses can be designed to meet their needs and assessment can be relevant and appropriate. We need to take into account not just their level,

but their reasons for joining the class, their preferred learning styles, and their personalities. Some learners feel very uncomfortable 'performing' in front of the rest of the class whereas others may be all too keen to 'have a go'. We may be able to incorporate exercises that are relevant for a learner who is going to be doing business abroad, or for the grandmother who wants to be able to communicate with her daughter-in-law's family.

3　Learners should be involved in assessment, in evaluating their own progress, strengths and weaknesses, in grading themselves and one another and identifying their own learning goals. This will help them to become more independent learners. This is not, however, always easy for learners to do at first. An example of a form which can help them to develop the ability to do this is given below. It lists the learning objectives of a lesson and learners simply tick when they feel they have achieved them. They are also invited to add further information.

Topic: talking about myself and my family	**Name:**

Can you do the following?　　　　　　　　**Tick and add further information**

☐　I can say my name.

☐　I can say where I live.

☐　I can talk about my family.

☐　I can understand someone else talking about themselves, where they live, their family.

☐　I can understand someone asking questions about my name, my family, where I live.

☐　I can read and understand a short passage about someone, where they live and their family.

☐　I can write a short passage giving my name, where I live and my family.

☐　I can also …

☐　I need to work more on …

The above example helps learners to understand what they are supposed to be able to do. It also helps them to appreciate that competence will vary between the four skills by specifying each one in a separate statement. It is in any case good teaching practice at the beginning of lessons to share objectives – *this is what we're going to do* – and at the end of lesson to re-cap – *this is what we have done,* and to check that the learning objectives have been met by asking specific and not open questions. Questions such as *Do you understand?* or *Is everything okay?* give limited information. Few learners feel comfortable admitting to not understanding. A more focused question, such as *How do you ask for a single ticket to Vienna?* or *Ask me what my hobbies are*, according to the learning objectives of the lesson, will indicate to the tutor whether or not they have achieved the lesson's objectives.

It is relatively straightforward to specify the learning objectives of lessons at basic levels of language learning and for learners to pinpoint what they have learnt. It is more difficult to be specific, however, in advanced classes, often called 'Advanced conversation', which aim to build on existing high levels of knowledge and competence. It is still, however, important to do so, as these classes typically include a wide range of previous experience and knowledge, and it is the teacher's responsibility to support each individual in the development of their skills. Thorough preparation of the language that learners will need to be able to use in order to complete a task, followed by a series of tasks moving from carefully controlled and structured to more open-ended tasks will enable all the learners to progress. The incorporation of small-group work will give all learners the opportunity to work at their own level and to build their confidence. An example of the competences that advanced learners might display would be:

Topic: immigration	Name:

Can you do the following? **Tick and add further information**

☐ I know and can use the key vocabulary in this area.

☐ I can participate in a general discussion about this topic.

☐ I can understand the gist of conversations spoken at normal speed about this topic.

☐ I can understand the detail of a written text on this topic, with help from a dictionary or other reference sources.

☐ I can also/I need to work more on …

4   It is important to share with the learners marking criteria so that they understand what they are trying to achieve. This should include consideration of issues of accuracy – do we expect our learners to be grammatically correct, or is the focus on whether or not a sympathetic native speaker will understand what is being said? Learners who believe that accuracy is essential at all times may hesitate to answer a question if they are not sure of the gender of a word. Marking is a very sensitive issue that needs careful thought; a page covered in red ink is not very encouraging, and the learners may well not learn very much from it apart from the fact that they have not done very well.

Initial assessment leading to individual learning goals

The importance of getting to know learners as well as possible as soon as possible has been stressed above. Only by knowing our learners can the course be tailored to meet their needs. It is, however, not appropriate to walk into a first adult education lesson and inform the class that we are going to give them a test. This could create anxiety and an inappropriate atmosphere for what we hope will be a rewarding and enjoyable experience. The way it is approached is therefore crucial, as the initial stages of our courses will set the tone for the whole course.

Before the course begins

Clear, accurate pre-course information must be readily available to learners, to enable them to make an informed choice about the class they wish to join. This may not be the direct responsibility of the individual tutor, but the tutor will no doubt have an opportunity to contribute to pre-course marketing information. Titles of courses can also be helpful: 'Improvers' is not very clear; an explanation of different levels will give a better indication of the proposed content of a course. Teachers might find it useful to produce a leaflet or one side of A4 to explain what their course aims to achieve, and have this ready at enrolment to distribute. Learners who are dissatisfied with courses often say that the course is not what they thought it was going to be. The more informed they are before the course begins, the less likely they are to be able to make this criticism. The following is an example of a leaflet that will give enough information to potential learners to enable them to make an informed decision about whether or not they wish to enrol for the course.

Wilbraham Adult College Tutor: Maria Roberts	Italian for fun 10 weeks Tuesdays, 7–9 Start date: 25 April £45/£25 concessions
Previous experience required? None – this is a course for complete beginners	
Materials required? Pen and paper: all other materials provided by the college	
Examination? None	
Course outline A lively, informal and enjoyable introduction to Italian, with lots of different activities and a focus on speaking, listening, and Italian cultural background. The course aims to develop the confidence to understand and speak in various situations – meeting people, shopping, getting around, cafes and restaurants etc. It will provide a solid basis of vocabulary, pronunciation, and understanding of basic grammar, which could be used to move on to a higher level if required.	
What next? Continue to Level 2, which builds on the introductory level.	

At the beginning of the course

A combination of strategies will help the teacher to gain as full a picture as possible of the learners. This can be done by a mixture of learner self-assessment and tutor assessment, but it is important that these assessment techniques do not take over the whole of a first lesson. It is important that, at the end of the first lesson, learners go away able to do something that they could not do at the beginning of the lesson. While the teacher will no doubt be measuring learning whatever the activity being undertaken, learners will not want to feel that the whole of the lesson has been spent on assessment.

Activities to measure the learners' levels

These could include:

- **Giving the learners a straightforward form to complete about themselves.** This could be largely a tick-box task and should not take too long. Learners may wish to discuss their answers, either with the teacher or one another. Having completed it, it would be appropriate for the teacher and the learner to keep a copy.

Name:

1 **Why are you interested in learning a language? Please tick no more than three.**

☐ For holidays	☐ For an enjoyable evening out
☐ For work	☐ To meet people
☐ Because I have friends/relatives in the country	☐ To gain a qualification
☐ To keep my mind alert	☐ Other (please specify)

2 **What is your previous language-learning experience? (language, level, school experience, etc)**

3 **How confident do you feel about the following aspects of language learning?**

Activity	Confident	Fairly confident	Not very confident	Help!
Listening and understanding in class	☐	☐	☐	☐
Understanding in the country where the language is spoken	☐	☐	☐	☐
Understanding tapes	☐	☐	☐	☐
Speaking in front of the class or a whole group	☐	☐	☐	☐
Speaking in pairs/a small group	☐	☐	☐	☐
Reading aloud	☐	☐	☐	☐
Reading a magazine or short items such as letters	☐	☐	☐	☐
Reading a novel	☐	☐	☐	☐
Writing a postcard or letter	☐	☐	☐	☐
Writing an essay	☐	☐	☐	☐
Grammar	☐	☐	☐	☐
Spelling	☐	☐	☐	☐

4 **How do you like to learn?**

☐ Alone ☐ With one other person ☐ In a group ☐ From the teacher

■ **An ice-breaking activity.** This has many purposes, including encouraging learners to get to know one another and creating a relaxed atmosphere, but it also gives the teacher the opportunity to identify strengths and learners who may need particular types of support. These activities consist often of learners talking to their neighbours in pairs and exchanging personal information and their fears and hopes for the course. They then introduce their neighbour to the rest of the group. Learners with some years of experience in adult education may be asked something less straightforward, e.g. identify three things you have in common and three things that are different with your neighbour, or the task may be to go round the class asking as many people as possible for information. To prepare for this activity the teacher could produce a handout with questions to ask. Questions, in the target language, might ask the learner to find someone who:

– has lived abroad;
– has recently moved to this area;
– has been to France more than six times;
– likes sport (which one?);
– supports Manchester United;
– has three children;
– can play a musical instrument (which one?);
– has a French car.

A class for beginners would clearly have to be done in English, but some form of ice-breaking activity is important at the beginning of any course. The teacher then has the opportunity discreetly to make notes on individuals to help with future course planning. The time that this would take could be reduced if the teacher has a class list to hand with space for comments. Again, the teacher might want to tick against certain criteria or give numerical scores to denote level of proficiency in a particular area.

Name	Exchange personal information	Use of tenses	Range of vocabulary	Pronunciation	Accuracy	Comprehension	Fluency	Use of questions	
F. Butcher	✓✓	✓✓ ✓	✓	✓✓ ✓	✓	✓✓ ✓	✓✓	✓	V. gd
V. Wilson	✓	✓	✓✓	×	✓	✓✓	×	✓	Has villa in Spain
J. Proud	✓✓	✓✓	✓✓	✓	✓	✓✓	✓	✓	Needs Spanish for work
M. Rose	✓	×	✓	✓	✓	✓	✓	×	Nervous: lacks confidence
T. Brown	✓✓	✓	✓	✓✓	✓✓ ✓	✓✓	✓	✓	Already speaks fluent French
M. Trent	✓	×	✓	✓	✓	✓	×	✓	Did same course last year
J. Summer	✓✓	✓	✓✓	✓✓	✓✓	✓	✓	✓	Attending with friend R. Townsley
R. Townsley	✓	✓✓	✓✓	✓	✓	✓	✓	×	Sometimes won't be able to attend — works away. Give handouts?

Class: Spanish Level 2

Here we have a class list, the teacher has listed what is expected of the learners, and ticks can be quickly noted down while the learners are completing a task. The teacher may feel that this includes too many criteria against which the individuals can be assessed and may wish to simplify it further. There is space at the right-hand side for additional notes, which is usually helpful as some information will not fit comfortably into a pre-designed grid. This example is for an initial assessment of a class, but it can be used at any point in a course.

■ **A written task**. This should not be too long at the beginning of a course, and what it consists of will depend on the level of the learners. They may, for example, be asked to write down personal information about themselves, their motivation for attending the class, to write about what they did over the summer, what they are planning for the weekend etc. Again, this task has more than one purpose – for the tutor to start to get to know about each learner's linguistic knowledge and also to get to know about their individual learning goals.

The purpose of initial assessment

> *The purpose of the initial assessment of the learners is to inform the subsequent development of the course ... with regard to the specific requirements of the individuals within that group.*

The purpose of the initial assessment of the learners is to inform the subsequent development of the course, not only in terms of the scheme of work that is produced for the group as a whole, but with regard to the specific requirements of the individuals within that group. A number of elements will contribute to this process. First, **learner self-assessment** will play a role as with the help of the teacher they develop the ability to identify their own strengths and areas for development. Secondly, the scheme of work needs to allow for differentiation so that the needs of individuals can be catered for. A sample scheme of work which addresses **differentiation** is given on pp104-105 (from Ainslie and Purcell 2001: 9–10).

Thirdly, class lists as exemplified elsewhere in this chapter can be used on a week-by-week basis to **monitor and record progress** against the week's objectives. This should be complemented by creating regular opportunities to discuss with individual learners the progress they are making, the ways in which their individual needs may be changing and their proposed next steps. The challenge for the tutor of achieving this is that it is potentially very time-consuming, and one of the criticisms made of the increased focus on assessment is that it takes up too much class time. There are, however, ways in which the time allocated to this can be manageable. In at least one large adult education centre the classes now have an extra fifteen minutes of class time allocated to them each week specifically to allow time for a review with individuals of their individual learning goals. For those who do not have this luxury, however, with careful planning it is sometimes possible to organise a lesson so that for part of the time the learners are working independently of the tutor and the tutor takes time to review progress with individuals. This independent activity may, for example, be preparing role plays, working on individual projects, a workshop activity, a computer-based activity or a written exercise. Alternatively, one lesson every few weeks can be allocated to individual tutorials. If learners do homework, feedback on that can contribute to reviewing progress and setting future targets.

<table>
<tr><td colspan="2">

Level 1

Topic: *In a café/bar*
</td><td>

Aim: To enable learners to get themselves something to eat and drink when in a (French)-speaking country
</td></tr>
</table>

Core objectives

By the end of the topic **all learners** will be able to ask for something to eat and drink and pay for it. **Some learners will:**

- be able to ask for a greater range of items;
- have additional specific vocabulary according to their tastes;
- be accurate in use of gender;
- be able to use several expressions to ask for items.

	Content (core)	*Opportunities for differentiation*
1	Introduction to topic and key new vocabulary (basic items of food and drink – eight to twelve items in total depending on group and level of response). (Possible list: *un café, un thé, un vin rouge, un vin blanc, une bière, un hot dog, une pizza, un sandwich au jambon, un sandwich au fromage, une glace, des frites* – very common vocabulary with a number of cognates.)	Before giving learners new vocabulary, ask the class to give vocabulary they may already know.
2	Presentation and repetition of key new vocabulary with flashcards/objects, etc. (Add *vous désirez, je voudrais* here after initial presentation and practice.)	After choral repetition, ask better learners to produce the new vocabulary first, so that they can act as models for the others. • Encourage more able learners to produce longer utterances than the others. • Correct with sensitivity according to the level of the learner.
3	Listening comprehension exercise – dialogue in a bar. (Prepare by revision of '*c'est combien?*' and numbers practice and consolidation.)	Give learners choice about how they address the exercise, e.g.: (a) they will probably have a list of vocabulary either on the board/in their books/on a handout – suggest that if they don't need to, they could try to do the exercise without looking at the list; (b) prepare two listening exercises, one asking for boxes in a grid to be ticked, one requiring written responses in the language. If both exercises are on one handout, the choice can be made without learners drawing attention to themselves; c) alternatively, have an extra box at the end of the grid to give the opportunity for learners to add additional information.
4	Correction of listening exercise.	If correcting in class, ask easier questions of learners who may find more difficult questions challenging – save the difficult questions for more advanced learners. Write the answers on the board or OHP so everyone can check.
5	Reading comprehension exercise, e.g. a menu and a short dialogue in a café.	Have additional exercises for those who finish quickly, e.g. more than one menu, longer dialogue, with more vocabulary. Exercises should normally be graded in degree of difficulty – easier ones first. All learners will complete earlier exercises, but only some will do later ones.

	Content (core)	Opportunities for differentiation
6	Role play; in a bar, in pairs. Structured tasks based closely on new vocabulary introduced.	Have a list of key expressions at the bottom of the role-play sheet, but suggest that if they can the learners fold it over and do the role play without consulting the list. **or** Give more than one role play and learners progress through them or choose the one(s) they would like to try. Consider strategies when putting learners into pairs, e.g. same level together **or** putting learners together so that one can help the other. Tutor gives support by moving round group.
7	Feedback from role play.	Some pairs may be keen to 'perform' their role play in front of the rest of the class – others may be too inhibited to try. For these you could listen to them and give feedback while the rest of the group is still preparing. With enough encouragement they may in time become less inhibited about 'performing' in front of the others. Correct sensitively at the end of the exercise – picking up on key recurring errors without singling individuals out for correction.
8	Revision/recall of vocabulary; introduction of additional lexical items. (e.g. *c'est tout, un café crème, un café au lait, un jus d'orange, de l'eau, un verre de, une bouteille de, pression, qu'est-ce que c'est, une menthe à l'eau?* Introduce alternatives to *'je voudrais – avez-vous?, est-ce que je peux avoir?'*.)	Try to elicit vocabulary first, then negotiate additional expressions, e.g. ask learners if they have other drinks/snacks that they would particularly like to be able to ask for. Include cultural awareness here (e.g. describe *un croque monsieur, un citron pressé, un kir*, different prices at the counter and on the terrace, the aperitif.)
9	Listening/reading comprehension to practise wider range of vocabulary.	As in 3, 4 and 5 above.
10	Video clip of café/bar with associated tasks.	Some learners might need a handout of key vocabulary; others may be able to understand without extra help.
11	More complex role plays – in groups. Authentic/more extensive stimulus material (menus).	Some may need an alternative task, e.g. to repeat the basic role play in a pair; others may now be able to order a wider variety of items, to order for their friends and to ask for further information. Tasks could be more open-ended and, where appropriate, learners could be encouraged to develop them as they wish.
	'Homework'.	This may be learning vocabulary/preparing role plays/reading comprehension exercises. Discuss with learners how they might approach learning independently and develop study skills. Encourage them to be involved in making decisions about what will be the most useful type of activity for them. Learners could be encouraged to design menus for one another to use as stimulus material – preferably produced on computer. Or they may be able to find 'authentic' menus on the Internet. They may also already have menus from trips abroad that could be brought in for the group to use.

Oral work

This can be assessed during pair-work activities if the tutor prepares the learners, gives them time to practise and then, when they are ready, listens to them and assesses them. This is a very unthreatening way of assessing the learners and can be a part of the normal lesson. Preparation for the exercise could be a role play followed by a similar exercise conducted as an assessment activity. For example, learners do a role play in a restaurant as a practice activity and the second task is also a role play in a restaurant but based on a different venue and a different situation.

task one

Customer: You are in a restaurant with an elderly relative and have to order a meal for her. She likes fish and soup but does not like fruit or alcohol. Order a meal for yourself and her.

Ask if you can pay by credit card and if the service is included.

Waiter: There is no soup left and the only dessert is apple pie. Recommend the local red wine.

You only take Maestro cards, not Visa.

task two

Customer: You are in a restaurant with a vegetarian client (he eats cheese but not eggs). Order a steak, chips and salad for yourself and ask the waiter what is available for vegetarians.

Waiter: You have three vegetarian options: omelette, quiche and pasta with a cheese sauce.

A pair-work exercise may not always give both partners the opportunity to demonstrate the same learning objectives and roles may need to be switched to allow both to demonstrate what they have learnt.

An example of an exercise in which both partners are carrying out equivalent tasks is 'Arranging to meet'. Each partner has a diary with part of it completed and the partners have to agree on a time when they could meet. As an imaginary telephone exercise the partners will not see one another's diaries. Successful completion of this task will be that the partners agree correctly on the only time when they are both free. This could be recorded in their file and signed by the tutor as an example of evidence gathered.

person A

Lundi	Matin	Travail
	Après-midi	
	Soir	Cinéma avec José
Mardi	Matin	Travail
	Après-midi	Coiffeur
	Soir	Dîner avec Gilles
Mercredi	Matin	Shopping
	Après-midi	Visite chez Grand' mère
	Soir	
Jeudi	Matin	Piscine
	Après-midi	
	Soir	Télé

person B

Lundi	Matin	
	Après-midi	Travail
	Soir	Télé
Mardi	Matin	Marché
	Après-midi	Club de bridge
	Soir	
Mercredi	Matin	Travail
	Après-midi	Travail
	Soir	
Jeudi	Matin	Café avec Maman
	Après-midi	Dentiste
	Soir	Babysitting pour Jeanne

The above pair-work exercise can be repeated as a practice exercise and then an assessment exercise, simply by changing the diary entries.

A combination of the range of strategies identified above will ensure that the needs of the individual learners are taken into account and addressed effectively.

Integrating assessment into teaching and learning

The scheme of work above includes a number of points at which the learning that is taking place is being monitored, but it is being monitored unobtrusively and the learners would not consider that they were in any way being tested. Nevertheless, the teacher and the learners will be aware of how well they are progressing in relation to their own and the lesson's objectives. The general principle is that each time we teach a new learning objective – and we will usually have several in each lesson – we must incorporate an activity that will monitor whether or not our learners are able to demonstrate that they have achieved the learning outcome associated with that objective. Sometimes the monitoring will be of a very specific nature, but from time to time it will assess more globally our learners' achievement. For example, in a lesson introducing the past tense, we will monitor informally the acquisition of a very small number of new verb forms at several stages throughout a lesson. We will then at the end of the lesson assess all of the verb forms that have been introduced piecemeal during the lesson.

Planning assessment tasks

At certain points a more formal approach to assessment might be more appropriate, and this will generally be an assessment of more than a small number of verb forms. Whatever the degree of formality or informality, however, several factors need to be taken into consideration when planning assessment tasks that are to be integral to our teaching.

1   Learners must be absolutely clear about what is expected of them and the purpose of an assessment task. They must know what is being tested, how it is being tested and how it will be assessed.

2   The starting point for choices we make about how we are going to measure learning should be what we are aiming to teach our learners, i.e. tasks should be **'fit for purpose'** – an appropriate task to measure a particular learning objective. For example, if we want to check that our learners are able to get something to eat and drink in a restaurant, it is not appropriate to ask them to do a written exercise or a spelling test.

3   The task should be **fair** – we should not test something that has not been properly prepared. Most of us have at some point prepared learners to do a role play as an assessed exercise which involved the learners exchanging information, and given lots of preparation for answering the questions but hardly any for asking the questions. We are then surprised when the learners struggle with formulating questions – a task that in many languages is very challenging and needs a lot of practice! As tutors we are used to asking the questions and forget to incorporate into our lessons opportunities for the learners to practise doing the asking. It is, however, quite straightforward to include such exercises into our

classes: ***Now ask me ...***; ***Ask your neighbour ...***; or have a game of twenty questions from time to time.

4   Assessment tasks should normally reflect the sort of tasks that have already been carried out in class. For example, if we spend a lot of time doing oral work it is not appropriate for an assessment task to consist of a written exercise. A role play that has been used as a practice exercise can form the basis of an assessment task. If the tutor has not been using the target language as the normal means of communication in the class, it will be more difficult for the learners to perform successfully an assessment task which is presented entirely in the target language.

5   Assessment tasks should be **varied**. This is in order to cater for the different learning styles of our learners and for the fact that they will have different learning goals and needs.

6   Assessment tasks should not take up too much lesson time but should be undertaken **regularly**. This might mean that we have to be selective in what we assess at any one time, but if assessment tasks are included at regular intervals enough evidence will be given of progress being made. If we do not monitor our learners' progress at regular intervals we may not be aware of difficulties that they are encountering and will therefore not be in a position to remedy them.

7   The assessment tasks should be at **the right level**; if they are too difficult learners may indeed become demotivated because they will feel that they cannot do what they have been taught; if they are too easy they will serve little useful purpose. This is quite challenging, however, partly because there is usually a wide range of level and ability within an adult education class. It will probably therefore be necessary to include tasks at different levels, so that everyone can succeed at some of them but the more advanced learners can be stretched, or at least have an opportunity to go a bit further in what they produce. It is normally good practice to have easier exercises at the beginning of tests and then to progress to more challenging ones. A test of this type may be introduced to the learners by saying, for example, that you think that everyone will be able to do nos. 1–5, but that some may like to have a try at the later ones.

Alternatively, exercises can be introduced that allow learners to expand on what they produce. A structured role play could be given to learners, who are then encouraged to expand/take it further – teachers could prepare an additional sheet of instructions to enable learners to do this. A simple example of a grid which could be used to check comprehension of a listening exercise, and which would allow the learners to decide whether or not they wanted or felt able to demonstrate wider learning, would be to include an extra column for 'additional information'. The example below is an extract from a listening exercise based on a conversation at a ticket office.

Train destination	Time of arrival	Passengers	First or second class	Cost	Additional information
Toulouse	19.25	One adult and two children	Second	€126	Woman travelling with nephew and niece; is restaurant car on train

8 Tutors should have a **clear policy about marking**. Tutors can give ticks, marks out of ten, grades, pass/fail only, correct all errors, selected errors, give oral feedback and/or written feedback, or not give any mark at all, simply give oral or written comments. Some centres have a marking policy, which is helpful, particularly if learners move from one class to another and find a different system of marking in place. Whatever the decisions made about marking, however, it is important to explain to the learners the marking criteria and the reasons for them. As with so many aspects of teaching, the decisions made about how to mark will depend on the expected outcomes of a course. The key is to think first of what you want the learners to demonstrate that they are able to do. If teaching a particular tense, for example, the tutor may decide not to correct errors in written work that had nothing to do with the acquisition of that tense. If this is the case, learners need to be aware that there may be errors that have not been corrected. And if a written task does contain a lot of errors, teachers need to ask themselves whether or not the task set was too difficult – we should not be setting our learners up to fail. In oral work, it is often not appropriate to correct any error of pronunciation, as this can interrupt the flow of the learner struggling to communicate effectively. Sometimes a teacher decides to correct different learners according to their abilities. In oral work a strategy often applied is to repeat an answer given by a learner, correcting any errors without drawing attention to the mistakes in a way that could be embarrassing. If while the learners are doing an oral exercise the teacher keeps a notebook to hand to jot down errors that are being made, these points can be picked up with the whole class after the oral work has been completed.

It is preferable to mark positively rather than negatively – to award marks for what the learners can do and not deduct marks for the mistakes they have made. Marks may be awarded for communicating a message, with additional credit given for doing so accurately. If preparing learners for an examination, it is important to find out what the marking criteria are for the examination and generally to use those in marking learners' work. When giving feedback it is important to try to find something positive to say, and give learners clear suggestions for improvement. It is also good practice to ask the learners for their own assessment of their performance first.

Decisions also need to be made about who does the marking, and when. It can be the teacher, the learner, another learner, in class time, or after the class. All have their place, depending on the situation. Marking in class has the advantage of giving instant feedback, particularly of listening or oral tasks, but it can take up a disproportionate amount of class time. To minimise the time taken teachers sometimes prepare in advance a handout or an overhead transparency with the answers on. An important principle, however we assess, is to return marked work as soon as possible, as the feedback is of little value if it is not soon after the assessment task was carried out.

9 The production of **appropriate assessment tasks** is a challenging one; an exercise that may seem crystal clear to the writer may be totally incomprehensible to someone else. It is advisable, when devising assessment tasks, to produce an answer grid as well as a mark scheme as this can indicate flaws in the task. When it comes to formal testing, it is also a very good idea for teachers to meet together as teams to develop appropriate assessment strategies and tasks for their learners, to check one another's, and to consult published materials for ideas.

Evidencing and recording attainment and achievement

In order to monitor learners' progress effectively, attainment and achievement must be evidenced and recorded.

In an accredited course the recording of learners' progress may be a requirement, and many tutors are finding the recording of evidence extremely time-consuming. They are either spending a lot of their own time recording progress, time which they are probably not being paid for, or a lot of class time is being spent on recording rather than learning. To minimise the amount of time spent recording, careful thought needs to be given to planning how to do it. Decisions about how to keep records are best made within a team rather than on an individual basis – pro-formas can be centrally produced to help. Most tutors have mark sheets or a mark book and they can be used to record a lot of information. If there is not enough room to include a description of each of the assessment tasks, the tasks could be numbered so that the relevant information can be accessed easily. To monitor that assessment tasks cover all four skills, the mark book could be divided into different sections for each of the skills, and some tutors use different colours to indicate different sorts of information.

Many of our learners are more interested in their ability to communicate orally than in writing, yet many teachers find it very difficult to monitor oral proficiency and assessment can take a very long time. Evidence can however be produced by learners recording themselves on audio or video tape, which can then be inserted into a portfolio. This can be accompanied by the teacher's records of oral competence achieved, even if, because of time constraints, it is not always possible to make a recording. Evidence of a successful information gap exercise can be the inclusion in a file of the answers to the information that was required, answers that the learners and the teacher sign as having been acquired via the task set.

In order to check the progress that learners are making towards meeting their objectives, a simple form can be produced by the teacher with the learning objectives of the lesson listed and individual records kept of the progress of learners towards meeting these objectives. This should not take up too much time either to produce or to complete, and will be a useful part of the record-keeping process discussed below.

An example of a form could be:

Class: _____

Topic: _____

Name	Can ask for something to eat and drink	Understands key vocab in café	Can ask for the price	Can use and understand general expressions (hello, goodbye, how are you, etc)	Other comments
A. Brown	✔	✔	✔	✔	Good accent
P. Jones	✔	✔	✔	✔	Can also ask for bigger/ smaller
L. Smith	✔		✔	✔	Needs to extend range of vocabulary
S. Griffiths		✔	✔	✔	Understands well; lacks confidence speaking
J. Gaskell	✔	✔	✔	✔	

Learners should also take responsibility for recording their own progress. The production of a portfolio, which may be little more than a file with all their work in, including handouts prepared by the tutor, should enable them to monitor their own progress. They can be issued with their own forms, such as those exemplified above, which will specify the progress they are making towards meeting their objectives. The learners' files could also contain the course outline or other information provided at the beginning of the course. As some learners are better than others at keeping files in order, from time to time some lesson time should be devoted to monitoring and reviewing how they are being kept.

Strategies for success in accredited work

The challenge for many accredited courses is the amount of evidence that has to be collected to demonstrate each aspect of the course, as one example is usually not considered to be adequate to demonstrate the achievement of a learning outcome. Careful planning alongside the strategies discussed above will contribute to success in managing this process. The scheme of work should cross-reference the assessment requirements and the content of the course so that the accreditation requirements can be met (see Chapter 3, p43, for information on and a detailed example of a scheme of work). There are also, however, a number of steps to take that are specific to the accreditation process.

1   Policies within which teachers have to operate change from time to time; however, at the time of writing learners are able to attend courses without having to register for accreditation. If learners do not wish or need to be accredited, it should be possible for them to pursue their learning goals without being constrained by an examination.

2   If accreditation is to be offered, and the individual teacher can have a say in which type of accreditation is to be undertaken, the accreditation that most closely matches the learning objectives of the learners should be chosen. However, no accrediting body can ever meet the needs of all the learners in a group, and courses will then need to be very carefully planned to try to maintain a balance between the individual's learning needs and the requirements of the examining board. A differentiated approach is essential.

3   Information provided to learners at the beginning of their courses must be quite clear about the nature of the accreditation and the impact that this will have on the course.

4   Once again, teachers should work with other colleagues to plan together and share responsibilities and resources. It might be appropriate for teachers to assess one another's learners from time to time, to give learners the experience of being assessed by someone who is not the normal teacher.

5   Teachers must thoroughly research the requirements of the examination – detailed documentation and sample assessment questions will be available and should be studied with care – wherever possible learners should also be given copies of documentation. The objectives of the course should be carefully aligned with the accreditation requirements.

6   Schemes of work and lessons should be planned that will incorporate the type of activities that will be included in the

external assessments, so that learners can be thoroughly prepared (see Chapter 3, p48, for information on and an example of a lesson plan).

7   Teachers should try to avail themselves of opportunities to attend training days or meetings which will support them in preparing the learners for assessment.

Conclusion

In an era of regular inspection of courses, inspectors will be focusing on the quality of the experience for the learner rather than on the quality of the teaching. We can do a brilliant performance at the front of the classroom, but if the learners, or some of the learners, are not learning, the inspector will not be impressed. The strategies outlined above suggest ways in which the teacher can ensure that learning can be measured in both a formal and an informal way, without detracting from the quality of the learning experience. The key to success in language learning is motivation and one of the most motivating factors for learners is the experience of success; appropriate monitoring and the demonstration to learners that they are acquiring new skills and knowledge can harness and enhance their motivation and lead to greater confidence and greater success.

References

Ainslie, S. and Purcell, S. (2001) ResourceFile 4: *Mixed-ability teaching in language learning.* CILT.

Evaluation

■ Steve Mann

This chapter comes at the end of the book. It is funny how evaluation always gets left to the end, isn't it? Actually, it is typical. The course finishes, time to evaluate. End of the year, time to evaluate the year. In many ways, this chapter questions this end weighting. It takes the position that looking at evaluation as an ongoing part of what we do as language teachers may be more positive.

> **Evaluation as an ongoing process can be seen as part of the art of what we do, rather than the end part of what we do.**

The term evaluation is often associated with large scale pursuits to establish whether curriculum or language-learning projects can be judged successful in achieving their stated goals. Evaluation as described here is less concerned with large scale one-off evaluative events and instead puts forward a view of evaluation as necessary and ongoing.

Apart from the scale and timing of evaluation, we also need to ask the question – who is doing the evaluating? Is it something done by others, by outsiders, by managers or by inspectors? Or is it healthier to see evaluation as something that those involved in the language-learning process (teachers and learners) can, to some extent at least, demonstrate control over. In fact, evaluation comes to us naturally. We do it all the time. We are all reasonably comfortable with the everyday evaluative choices and decision making moments that life throws up.

Teachers don't make decisions about language-learning methodology on a whim; they make often complex decisions through an ongoing and everyday series of evaluations. Those teachers that learn to enjoy the challenge of teaching a foreign language do so because they are, for the most part, rather adept at evaluation. What I want to do here is to investigate further what is often a relatively informal and ongoing process. I want to consider ways to make it more explicit within the process of language learning and teaching analysed in this book from different angles. Evaluation can become a reflective process that is shaped by the participants (learners and teachers).

Four perspectives

In evaluating language teaching activities, methodologies, courses and materials, there are important perspectives that need to be taken into account. This chapter looks at evaluation from four perspectives, which allows us to consider the views of various parties and stakeholders.

- Learner evaluation
- Self-evaluation
- Peer evaluation
- Outsider evaluation

Each of the four views has a part to play in providing different forms of information and evidence for reflection and development. The first three viewpoints are internal ones. External evaluators are very unlikely to have the kind of grasp on the methodology, courses and materials that internal participants will have. Each of these viewpoints has nonetheless a part to play in shaping and re-energising the teaching and learning process in order to achieve individual or collective learning outcomes. In essence, what good evaluation is concerned with is using multiple perspectives. Mapping a number of evaluative angles strengthens any account and makes it more reliable. Often richer evaluation looks less at measurement and prediction and more at description and interpretation.

Testing, assessment and evaluation

I want to stress at this point a difference between the term assessment and the term evaluation. Simply, it is possible to evaluate teaching without relying solely on testing learners' language. A test certainly is one way of evaluating the effectiveness of teaching. However, it is not the only form of evaluative evidence that counts. Unfortunately, it is at times the only kind of evaluative data that some teachers collect.

One of the reasons why assessment often gets centre-stage is that policies and practices in language teaching programmes have increasingly pushed teachers to provide much more explicit information on programme activities and outcomes. It is also the case that recent years have seen a return, in all sectors of education, to calls for more teacher-conducted assessments as a basis for reporting learners' progress and achievement against national standards. This 'push' means that teachers are finding themselves in the position of having to develop tools and procedures for recording, reviewing, monitoring, and assessing learners' progress and achievement in educational settings on a more systematic and formal basis.

Learner evaluation

The first perspective on evaluation is the learner perspective. There may be reasons why teachers are reluctant to encourage learner evaluation and I will discuss some of the possible concerns that language teachers have in what follows, as well as suggest some strategies to address them. However, it is certainly the case that inspectors value and seek out the learner perspective as expressed in the *Common Inspection Framework* published by the Office for Standards in Education (OFSTED) and the Adult Learning Inspectorate (ALI):

> *'Inspections will focus primarily on the experiences and expectations of individual learners ...'*

Seeking learner evaluation has become increasingly mainstream. Published textbooks and learner resources, e.g. Ellis and Sinclair, Baxter, have explored ways in which learners can be encouraged to

> *Learners are increasingly encouraged to share the responsibility for successful language learning.*

evaluate their own learning. A number of writers have described this shift as a change in the responsibilities for both teachers and learners. The teacher is expected to relinquish some control over aspects of the education process and involve learners in their learning.

Barriers or constraints to learner evaluation

There may be barriers or constraints at work in asking for learner opinion or eliciting evaluative comment (see Sharp 1990: 135 for more on 'barriers'):

- asking a learner about your course may suggest that you don't know what you're doing. They may not see it as their concern;
- learners may not always give an honest reply. They may tell you what they think you want to hear;
- a level of distrust or antagonism may exist in some teacher-learner relationships;
- the relationship might be in the early stages of development;
- learners may feel that adverse comment may have some negative effect on their grade and so may only be comfortable giving positive evaluations.

There may also be other barriers. For example, with beginners in particular, if the teacher is not as proficient in the learners' native language, it may be difficult to involve them in the evaluative process. Conversely, the teacher's proficiency in the learners' native language can help build up an informal evaluative view.

In heterogenous classes, the most commonly found scenario in the field, there may be a wide variety of experience with regard to involvement with evaluation. In addition, learners who experienced predominantly the traditional teacher-led learning modes, may feel that evaluation is primarily the preserve of the teacher. Cross-cultural and cross-generational issues and different expectations may cause strong mismatches (see Makarova & Ryan).

Introducing learner evaluation

You do not have to be too ambitious at first. A good place to start is simply by getting learners to discuss things in class rather than by resorting to more formal questionnaire surveys. Parrot is a worthwhile and sensible starting point because the evaluative tasks in his book are small scale and can be done **while** you are teaching. They offer focused discussion, if the idea of a more general discussion worries the teacher.

> *Learners may be able to provide useful feedback on what is happening in the classroom.*

The recognition of the value of learner feedback has arisen with the increasing focus on learner autonomy, self-directed learning, self-access systems and individualised/independent learning in second language-learning literature. As Anita Wenden says:

> *'Few teachers will disagree with the importance of helping language learners become more autonomous as learners'* (1991: 11).

There is a reciprocal relationship between such concepts, i.e. a learner who cannot self-evaluate will not have the understanding necessary to give useful feedback. It is not possible to increase learner autonomy without introducing self-evaluation.

Research supports the view that learners have the ability to provide meaningful input into the assessment of their performance, and that this assessment can be valid. It also reveals high correlations between self-assessment data and data based on external criteria (see e.g. Blanche).

Learner self-assessment has now been well established as an important part of managing learning. However, at the same time as putting self-assessment at the centre of things, we need to:

- **build up a fuller profile of the learner** – The following affect the ability to engage in self-assessment: Language needs, motivation for language learning, amount of previous exposure to the target language and/or prior learning, learning of other languages, age, training in, or experience of, self-assessment;
- **give learners the necessary language** – To be able to evaluate their performance, learners need to know, in simple and practical language, exactly what it is that they are trying to evaluate;
- **understand that some skills are harder to self-assess than others** – It may be possible for learners to assess their own fluency and reading level – whereas pronunciation and accuracy in grammar may be much harder to self-evaluate.

Profiling and checklists

Ideally, the learner should be part of the process of recording and checking.

As well as building up a learner profile based on the kind of information above, one of the ways of recording and evaluating a learner's language learning is to build up a profile over time with the involvement of the learner. The profile can include statements of self-assessment and individual learning outcomes.

In addition to developing profiles, checklists can be helpful in keeping auditable records. Colin, talking about using checklists, sees this process as essential in improving learner confidence and involvement:

The checklists we have developed this year encourage learners to assess their confidence in different areas of the course. We've tried to make them more regular and less dauntingly long. Little and often. Most of us feel that they're helping to build confidence, self-assessment skills and guide.

He also sees them as helping learners to see progress and identify aspects of the course that they feel are useful. Of course they don't always come on in leaps and bounds, but if there is a sense of progress in the scores, the learners begin to see it over time.

If we were to list all the aspects of language teaching that could be evaluated, it would have to be a long list. However, some important areas would need to be included, such as:

- effectiveness of the course for learners;
- balance of activities;
- perceived language gains;
- missing skills and strategies;
- unpredicted learning;
- task evaluation (how the task was performed, what language was used, what learning took place, teacher and learner opinions of the task). Task evaluation has a habit of ballooning out and revealing other issues.

Teachers increasingly use video or audio recording of learner conversations to encourage self-evaluation. They explore numerous ways to use the recordings to point out a variety of target conversation strategies such as feedback phrases, conversation gambits, and ways of dealing with problems (e.g. asking for repetition).

It is the capacity of formative evaluation to shape and enhance practice that I want to stress:

> *'Formative evaluation is ongoing in nature, and seeks to form, improve, and direct the innovation, rather than simply evaluate the outcomes.'* (Williams and Burden 1994: 22)

The teacher can encourage evaluation from learners. Talking about classroom issues provides a ready made and shared context. It is as legitimate as talking about food and drink or travel, to name but two of our ubiquitous textbook themes. At its simplest, in such discussions learners are asked real questions as part of everyday language teaching methodology, which involves them in on-going evaluation. Examples of such 'real questions' would be:

- Were the materials useful?
- What have they learned?
- What was difficult?
- Which aspects of a text/dialogues/video clip, etc were interesting?

It is important to record and keep some of the learner answers/comments. Not only do we know that inspectors like to see that teachers have encouraged and kept examples of learner voices – especially if such examples are integrated into reports and summaries of successful teaching – but more importantly, analysis of cumulative evaluative records allow teachers to further individualise learning objects according to the varying degrees of progress within a group.

Encouraging the evaluative perspective of learners is possible in all aspects of teaching reading, writing, speaking and listening skills and it might be useful to finish with an example of a teacher who has encouraged learner comment and arrived at a shared summary.

Martin involved his learners in talking about how writing should be evaluated by both him as teacher and in peer-evaluation. This piece of action research established some key points for the class in the giving of evaluation.

- Learners felt more comfortable with feedback if the evaluator starts and ends comments with something positive. One learner said he 'felt relief if the first words are positive'.
- General comments are not as useful as specific ones where an example is pointed to in the text.
- It is better if feedback reinforces what has been emphasised in class. This helps use the same terminology and stress the same issues.
- Too much feedback is daunting for learners. There is only so much that learners can concentrate on. It is better to focus on three or four significant issues, even if that means leaving others uncovered.
- Written comments, on homework for example, need to be clear and easy to read.

Self-evaluation

Action research, reflective practice and the insider view

As well as a recognition of the value of the learner perspective, in the last few decades there has been a steady growth in the appreciation of action research which puts the language teacher, as a professional, at the centre of things. This might be contrasted with outsider or 'expert' research. In the latter, typically, the outsiders arrive to evaluate the strengths and weaknesses of an institution or programme. They come in, they make their pronouncements and they leave. This kind of outsider evaluation is inevitable and usually unavoidable.

Of course the language I am using is loaded. It is too easy to stereotype the outsider as some unfeeling judge rather than an interested observer wanting to help maintain or even raise standards. The argument I want to make here is that developing your skills in encouraging learner evaluation, self-evaluation and peer-evaluation will prepare you better. Whereas an outsider evaluator is more likely to offer a 'fresh' perspective and may give the evaluation credibility, the teacher will be able to bring an insider's perspective to the evaluation, complete with an awareness of local particularities, trends over time, etc.

Developing the insider view

The idea that the inside view is a valuable one in evaluative terms is not a new one. It has been established in the last few decades with accounts of language teaching practice that might be grouped under the headings 'action research' and 'reflective practice'. The main themes that emerge from these movements are:

- the insider view is crucial to understanding the complex world of the classroom and the nature of language learning;
- this complex world is simply not reducible to causal statements;
- a committed language teacher employs a continual process of reflection on practice.

A process of self-evaluation through reflection and action research has the capacity to reveal the kind of 'invisible' knowledge that is part of our everyday routines.

Self-evaluation through reflection and action research can reveal our experiential knowledge which is ingrained. Many of our successful teaching behaviours are unconscious. This is why video taping a class or peer observation are powerful ways to reveal this invisible knowledge.

Naidu et al talk of 'recovering experience' through a process of self-evaluation in order to improve practice. They also affirm that as teachers we ...

> '... possess a vast repository of classroom experience, which when shared with other teachers can lead to a body of theoretical insights and practical procedures.' (1992: 162)

Making the invisible more visible and conscious is the first step in an evaluative process which can result in sharing practical experience, information and best practice. If it is documented, then it provides an audit trail of such evaluation and dissemination of good practice.

Being involved in self-directed evaluation can contribute considerably to teacher development. The process can lead to a 'deepening and development of teachers' perceptions of classroom events', developments in language teaching practice, 'improved dialogue with peers', and improved skills and motivation for exploring and talking about issues of professional concern (see Weir and Roberts 1994: 7–8).

Plausibility

Action research offers the chance to develop your evaluative understanding or what has been called a sense of plausibility. This is teachers' subjective understanding of the teaching they do. It is a teacher's working assumptions of what is happening in the classroom and how teaching leads to desired learning.

Action research might well arise out of discussion with your learners. It is a good idea to start with such small scale investigation. (Parrot is a good place to start because the research tasks in his book are small scale and typically done with learners and while you are teaching.) Once you have decided on an idea to investigate and evaluate, the next important challenge is to narrow the focus as soon as possible. In other words, it is important to consider how a 'general issue' can be made more manageable.

Narrowing the focus

My experience, in working with teachers in a variety of contexts, is that they have little problem in finding a 'general issue' but that this issue or problem is often too big and, therefore, daunting and demotivating. Achieving a focus, small enough to manage, which does not 'balloon up' and become overwhelming, is where focusing circles and mind-mapping might be useful.

Focusing circles

This is a technique from Edge (1992: 37–8) in which you can narrow down your focus by drawing a small circle at the centre (inside) of a larger one. The issue, topic or problem is written in the small circle and the larger one is divided into four segments. In each of these segments an aspect of the topic is written. One of these four segments then becomes the centre of the next circle and so on.

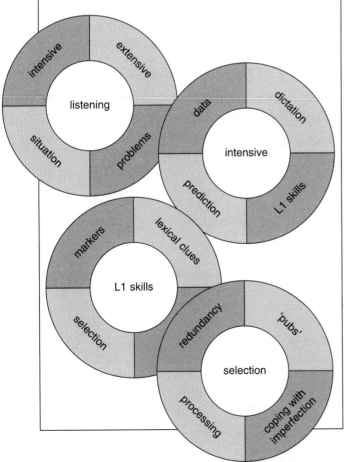

Mind maps

Most teachers have, at some time, used mind maps or 'spider webs'. Probably the most comprehensive guide to the use of mind mapping is provided by Buzan. Here the issue is written at the centre of a piece of paper and related factors branch out from the centre.

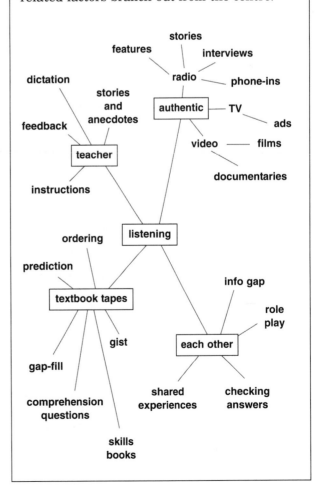

Teachers report that there is a different kind of thinking involved in the two techniques. The thinking in focusing circles *'is selective ... you are involved in deciding ... you need to make choices and justify them'*. In mind maps *'the main thinking goes into making connections, one thing leads to another'*. Most teachers feel that, of the two, focusing circles is more productive in finding a focus for action research. Once a decision has been made (i.e. a focus found), then mind mapping can be used to trace back the connections and see the 'small focus' within the 'bigger picture'.

Getting the focus right for your first piece of action research is very important because these early experiences shape your attitude and commitment to further action research. Try to avoid topics or questions that are essentially unanswerable. Also (see Burns 1999: 55):

- avoid questions you can do little about;
- limit the scope and duration of your research;
- try to focus on one issue at a time;
- choose areas of research which are of direct relevance and interest to yourself and to your school circumstances.

If you start with a problem which you want to solve, do not be too ambitious. In other words, do not choose a problem for which the solution may be beyond your scope. It is a good idea to think of teaching as a puzzle which you can explore, rather than a difficulty which needs to be solved. Consequently, it is suggested that your first piece of action research focuses on a puzzle or a small change in your classroom practice rather than diving in and trying to solve your biggest problem with your most difficult class.

Collecting data

In terms of collecting data that might be added to portfolio statements or records of self-evaluation, the most obvious starting point is keeping a diary or journal. Alternatively, a folder of memos may be more possible because these can be written in class and make less of a demand on teacher time. These informal notes can become records of thinking and reflection, especially if they point to changes in methodology or materials and are followed by action.

Various forms of data collection can inform a process of ongoing self-evaluation. Here is a list of some practical ways to collect data:

- classroom notes (perhaps on 'post-its');
- self-monitoring memos;
- reflection summaries (usually after the lesson) maybe recorded on the lesson plan;
- tapes of classes (audio or video);
- class discussions (perhaps with an OHP or interactive whiteboard summary);
- post task feedback (learner notes);
- information from learners (surveys/questionnaires).

Portfolios

A great deal of what is suggested in this chapter can be fed into what is usually termed a 'portfolio'. In recent years more teachers, like artists or architects, have started to keep such a portfolio of their work and ideas. These portfolios are samples of professional plans, lessons, ideas that demonstrate development of teaching skill. Portfolios are becoming a common way of communicating information about best practice to others as well as helping the individual language teacher understand his or her own teaching better.

Peer evaluation

So far, we have looked at opportunities for collecting evaluative viewpoints from learners and from the individual teacher, through a process of action research and reflective evaluation. However, to end the chapter at this point would be to reinforce the stereotype that teaching is a lonely and unsupported business. One of my colleagues once said *'teachers don't have colleagues, just people who work in the same place'*. There is an element of truth in this for a number of teachers who often lack the opportunity and scope for peer support. Other teachers work in isolation or disparate communities and I want to consider how peer evaluation could be adapted to a 'distance collaborative relationship'.

Peer co-operative development (CD)

> *Sharing ideas with colleagues is one of the most important ways in which teachers support each other.*

Most teachers simply don't get enough time for sharing ideas with colleagues. Teachers' meetings are often dominated by extensive agendas and are rarely conducive to sharing ideas. Language teachers have wide classroom experience and when this experiential knowledge is shared with other teachers, it feeds an evaluative process that can provide insights and practical procedures. However, this is not the same as saying that when a teacher describes a difficulty or challenge with a particular language class that peer advice, suggestions and evaluation will necessarily be helpful. Responses like *why don't you try...* or *there's a good activity in...* or *I find that...* are typical of the quick exchanges that happen in a break in the staffroom. They don't necessarily solve the problem but they are an important part of the social currency of teacher exchange and support.

In what follows I am not saying that such informal swapping of ideas and quick fixes are not helpful. Rather, I am suggesting that peers can work together in more sustained and developmental ways that keep the attention on the ideas of the individual teacher in his or her attempt to move thinking forward.

Time put aside for teachers to articulate their practice in the presence of peers can be useful. Edge (1992, 2002) provides a framework for peers to work together so that an individual teacher can work on an issue or concern and make progress. This can be done face-to-face or by phone, e-mail or on-line chat.

The way of 'talking' offered in CD provides a way in which teachers can:

- increase awareness of their own teaching strengths and skills;
- add an appreciation of the strengths and skills of others;
- create a willingness to listen carefully to others;
- provide an ability to respond appropriately to the needs of their own teaching situation.

In essence, what is on offer here is a way of talking to each other which encourages the teacher to be open and results in greater possibilities for articulation and eventual integration of ideas. I have used this way of talking with several other language teachers and have found it an enjoyable and useful way to develop my thinking.

CD procedures

This is a way of talking that can be done in small groups or pairs. One of the group acts as Speaker and the others act as Understanders. The conversation proceeds as follows:

Reflecting	Trying to say back a version or part of what the Speaker has just said. This both helps the Understander show that they understand the Speaker's ideas and also allows the Speaker a chance to hear a version of their account coming back.
Focusing	Here the Understander picks out one element of what the Speaker has said and offers it back to the Speaker. An example of this might be if the Understander says 'you said ... would you like to say any more about that?'
Thematising	Here the Understander picks out two or more elements of what the Speaker has been saying and offers the speaker the chance to articulate their relationship. An example of this would be if the Understander says ' you have talked about ... (A) ... and ... (B) ..., do you see a connection between them?'

The normal way of talking is changed to allow more space for the speaker to provide a fuller account of the way in which he or she teaches. It is a way for teachers to talk themselves into a fuller understanding and evaluation of just what it is that they do in the classroom. It creates extra room for the kind of self-evaluation described in the previous section.

Peer observation

I'm going to use the term peer observation rather than the just as widely used terms peer review and peer evaluation. Observation is perhaps a more neutral term. It may well **lead** to evaluative processes, but it offers at least the possibility that comment might be made which is simply a statement of what happened in the class rather than the suggestion of what should have happened. Again, it can be structured in such a way as to leave the evaluative role primarily with the teacher rather than the observer. So, it can be a case of helping the teacher to re-enter interesting moments in the lesson, and perhaps assisting in recall. Being clear about what actually happened is often the best starting point for building the kind of trust necessary for such a process to be useful in more evaluative terms.

We also need to make a distinction between peer observation and other more hierarchical observations. These might include:

- **mentoring** – a system for supporting new or less experienced members of staff;
- **appraisal** – a management (top-down) system for assessing practice and performance;
- **discipline** – a system for dealing with serious and persistent under-performance.

A badly run observation, review or evaluation scheme runs the risk of cutting down on dialogue, reinforcing institutional hierarchies, and risks poisoning otherwise productive working relationships among school professionals.

Benefits

Why get involved in peer observation? Collaborative peer observation can provide opportunities for teachers to learn how to consider and reflect on how to teach more effectively, to practise new teaching techniques and approaches. It can also help get peer feedback on their classroom performance, and to receive feedback from colleagues.

There are benefits (Cosh) both for the observing and the observed teacher, in that it can help to:

- improve the quality of the learning experience for language learners;
- promote and support a process of professional development and, possibly, action research;
- provide data for the observed teacher to identify their own strengths and areas for improvement;
- encourage a process of inner dialogue and reflection on teaching practice;
- encourage a process of dialogue between teachers and to identify and examples of innovation and best practice;
- provide evidence of best practice and quality teaching performance;
- assist in preparations for external quality review and inspection.

However, such schemes need to be voluntary. There are several reasons why teachers might not want the 'intrusion' of observation. It can be disruptive and can be seen as an infringement on teaching freedom. Indeed, most accounts of peer-evaluation stress the importance that the process be a mutual, collaborative and supportive one. It should not be hierarchical and judgmental.

Making the peer's role a non-evaluative one can be a way of making the idea less threatening because, normally, a peer-observation without evaluation is a rare event.

Training packages and workshops

Probably the best bet for language teachers who are involved in setting up a peer-observation scheme is to choose a peer-observation package explicitly aimed at language teachers. Beigy and Woodin's *Tandem observation: developing excellence in language teaching through the observation of peers* is a very usable resource which lays out the main issues involved and shows examples of language teachers working and interacting together. Tandem Observation emphasises the supportive, reciprocal and non-hierarchical nature of observations for development purposes. It introduces reflective practice in observation of teaching to teachers who are unfamiliar with the practice and structure of peer observation. Such materials are particularly useful if you are considering an institutional observation scheme. This package also has some useful accompanying support materials. The booklet *Developing skills in teaching languages* (Beigy and Woodin) is also full of techniques for stimulating language learning.

Getting the evaluation element right

The most important issue with peer-observation is to decide how evaluative you want the process to be. The following is a list of suggestions for getting the evaluation right.

- Allow the teacher to make the early comments. The teacher could describe the class and comment on how they felt the lesson went before the observer makes any evaluative comment. The teacher might, for example, reflect on whether being observed has altered the class in anyway.
- The observer's early comments should be positive if possible. Statements about what the observer considers the teacher to have done with competence, care, awareness and skill need to come before any 'constructive criticism'. Just as with potentially negative evaluation, positive evaluation needs to be backed up by evidence or instances of any claims made. If not, comments may seem insincere.
- Only after positive comment should the observer start to identify what did not appear to go well, comment on specific difficulties or areas of concern. Particular examples and instances will help keep the discussion centred on the interaction between teacher and learners. In this phase, it is important that the teacher has the chance to articulate this or her viewpoint of any difficulty, perceived weakness or concern.

Setting up a workable framework for peer observation

As well as being voluntary and reciprocal, collaboration on a process of peer observation is widely felt to be best structured using a three-phase model (see Fullerton). There is:

- **pre-observation** – used to discuss the class, lesson plan, the aim of the observation and a task for the observer to accomplish
- **observation** – carried out using the procedures that both teachers have agreed upon
- **post-observation** – the two teachers meet to report on information collected or discuss areas outlined in the pre-observation session.

Video-taping can be used as more than just an alternative to peer-observation and can have a complementary role. Video-taping of classes has a unique potential in identifying particular moments in the classroom for close observation and improved recall. It is a way of documenting and preserving the strengths of teachers as well as identifying weaknesses. It can also be added to teacher portfolios. In fact, with advances in the use of digital cameras and easy-to-use digital editing softwares like 'i-movie', teachers can assemble much more easily examples of good practice, for sharing ideas, evaluation and preparing for inspection.

Outsider evaluation

The argument so far is that a process of:

- encouraging evaluative comment from learners;
- engaging in self-evaluation;
- exploring the role peers can play in the evaluative process;

will put you in a strong position not only for dealing with outside evaluation, but also provide you with a coherent framework within a language department to standardised teaching and quality assurance approaches. Developing as many perspectives as you can not only gives you the views of the different stakeholders, but it allows you to develop a richer and more multi-perspective view point.

The role and concerns of those with the task of inspecting you in conjunction with, and taking account of, your departmental or organisational self-assessment report is outlined in documents such as *The Common Inspection Framework, Interpreting the Common Inspection Framework,* and *The Handbook for Inspecting Colleges* which make very clear what is to be inspected and how. They are downloadable from the ALI and OFSTED websites (see Appendix, pp134–135). The Inspectorates also give extensive advice on how to prepare for inspection. However, some common themes do emerge and these form the basis of this section.

> *Inspectors are looking for evidence of sustained and long-term development of learners, teachers, courses and language-learning provision.*

There is probably a great deal that can be achieved in the few weeks leading up to an inspection, but what the inspectors are looking for is evidence of sustained and long-term development of learners, teachers, courses and language-learning provision. It is therefore worth thinking and talking about these matters well before an inspection is timetabled. The usual amount of notice for an inspection is two months. Encouraging the three evaluative perspectives previously outlined in this chapter will be an important ongoing preparation, but they cannot be introduced two months before an inspection.

What inspectors are looking for is a process of continuous improvement. Indeed, the whole rationale of inspections is to be part of a cyclic process of:

- self-evaluation;
- development-planning and target-setting;
- monitoring and reviewing the extent to which plans are achieved and targets are met;
- sharing good practice;
- external inspection.

The Common Inspection Framework

The *Common Inspection Framework* is a document that recognises that it is necessary for the two inspectorates (ALI and OFSTED) to agree upon the terms on which their inspections are conducted. It is easy to read but some of the categories have a rather 'catch-all' quality. It is short on detail, perhaps because that is what you are expected to provide!

As far as possible in this chapter I have tried to use the important terms of the *Common Inspection Framework*:

Provider
Any organisation involved in providing education and training, including colleges, training providers and Local Education Authorities (LEAs).

Learner
A person receiving education or training, including student, trainee, apprentice, client and participant.

Teacher/trainer
Someone responsible for teaching or training. As well as those specifically referred to as teachers or trainers, the term includes lecturers, tutors, instructors, supervisors, technicians and assessors when they have a teaching or training function, and others involved in providing learning support.

Learning goals
These can take a variety of forms including single qualifications, groups, modules or units of qualifications, greater knowledge, competence and skills, milestones towards qualifications or employment, or securing employment, or a place in higher or further education.

Personal and learning skills
These include communication, presentation and teamwork skills, independent study, research and analytical skills.

The framework includes the more specific evaluation requirements that apply to the inspection of individual providers of education and training. In summary, they are looking at issues of quality and value for money:

- the quality of education and training;
- the standards achieved by learners receiving that education and training;
- whether financial resources made available to those providing that education and training are managed efficiently and used in a way which provides value for money.

Given that one of their stated aims is to '*help bring about improvement by identifying strengths and weaknesses and highlighting good and poor practice*', developing the three evaluative perspectives above can provide important data for their evaluation. It can demonstrate improvement and provide information to help highlight good practice, as well as document a commitment by the organisation to quality assurance, monitoring of the quality of teaching and learning and continuous improvement.

Right at the beginning of this chapter we said that inspections focus primarily on the experiences and expectations of individual learners. Inspectors will be looking at:

- what is achieved – the standards reached and learners' achievements, taking account of their prior attainment;
- the quality of teaching, training and learning;
- other aspects of provision that contribute to the standards achieved, such as the range, planning and content of courses or programmes, resources, and the support for individual learners;
- the effectiveness with which the provision is managed, its quality assured and improved, and how efficiently resources are used to ensure that the provision gives value for money;
- the extent to which provision is educationally and socially inclusive, and promotes equality of access to education and training, including provision for learners with learning difficulties or disabilities.

Although *The Common Inspection Framework* is a good place to start, there is no shortage of information that can also feed into your discussion in preparation for outside evaluation.

It would be impossible to provide a complete picture of all the organisations who can support the development of a coherent policy for furthering continuing professional development and preparing for outside evaluation. However, I have listed a selection of useful organisations in the Appendix (pp134–135).

What will inspectors be looking for?

In answering this question think about whether your learners have been set targets. Consider who has set these targets. It is likely that this will be a mix of learner goals and group goals. You might also consider how often learners are given a chance to evaluate their work in relation to any learning goals.

Inspectors are increasingly likely to take context into account. Not only will they look at the institutional context in which learning is taking place, but they will also consider how well learners have progressed relative to their prior attainment and potential. Inspectors are interested in how well learners learn and make progress, but they are also interested in obstacles to this progress. In particular, they will be interested in the adequacy and use of specialist equipment, learning resources and teaching rooms.

Part of an inspector's assessment of learners' progress will be an evaluation of the types of assessment, monitoring and evaluation that are taking place. They will want to know how well the programmes and courses meet the needs and interests of learners. Evaluation of course design goes hand in hand with how learners perceive and react to the courses.

One crucial element of an inspection is the judgment of how well learners are guided and supported. Inspectors will look at the quality of information, advice and guidance to learners in relation to the courses and programmes they are following. They will be looking for evidence that there is diagnosis of, and provision for, individual learning needs. In addition they will want to see evidence that the whole person is being catered for. Consequently, they will want to see provision of effective support on personal issues.

Inspectors are looking to highlight those teachers who are making a valuable contribution to improvement and are always happy to see more information and other materials than demanded. In a short visit, there is a limit to the 'evidence' that can be gathered from observations, from learners, from staff and others. As inspectors are required to come up with secure judgments, an audit trail of the three processes described above will certainly have impact and feed into their evaluation.

Well kept records of such evaluative processes will undoubtedly influence inspectors' thinking according to their seven-point scale by highlighting the concerted approach to aspects of quality assurance in the spirit of an organisation-wide strive to continually improve its provision. It is often a small margin between the award of one grade and another. The kind of evaluative work suggested in this chapter can certainly mean the difference between say a grade 3 (good) and a grade 2 (very good) and would give you a chance of achieving a top grade.

Inspectors' reports

As well as considering the questions and concerns that inspectors might have when coming to your institution, one of the most obvious but important things you can do is to:

- get hold of copies of inspection reports. Look particularly at the sections on 'English, languages & communications' (learning area 13);
- contact other colleges and organisations in your area who have been inspected. ALI will be able to help you in this quest.

The best place to start looking at inspection reports is the ALI website. As the inspection process is an open process, there are records of all inspections. If you do print off some of these inspection reports, look for common comments that emerge. A quick look through the 'key weaknesses' may give you some idea of what you might need to strengthen, e.g. you might see comments like:

- weak curriculum management;
- incomplete quality assurance arrangements;
- inadequate assessment processes.

In the 'key strengths' section you might see comments like:

- good achievement of personal objectives by learners;
- strong provision of learning support.

Make a list of such key comments and use them as the basis for your initial diagnosis of what weaknesses you need to take account of and how you can build on your key strengths.

As I said above, each teaching context is different. Teachers and learners are different. It is impossible to provide a recipe for inspection success to fit all contexts, but the suggestions above will help you strengthen your position for inspection.

Conclusion

This chapter has outlined four evaluative perspectives. Each teaching context will vary in the extent to which all four perspectives can be sought and developed simultaneously. However, any attempt to go beyond a reliance on assessment as the main form of evaluation is bound to help both learners and teachers.

My experience is that these evaluative perspectives are complementary. Interesting developments in one perspective leads naturally to interesting developments in another. In most cases, seeking the learner's evaluative perspectives is the best first step. What learners have to say almost inevitably leads to fine-tuning classroom procedures. Such changes are often communicated to peers and become part of a healthy professional development and sharing of good practice.

Evaluation is potentially a beginning. It can be a new start in finding out more about the complex business of language teaching. If it involves all the main stakeholders, it has more chance of building up a convincing overview of this complex world.

References

Ainslie, S. (1994) *Mixed-ability teaching: meeting learners' needs.* CILT.

ALI and OFSTED (2001) *The common inspection framework for inspecting post-16 education and training.*

Anson, C. M. (1994) 'Portfolios for teachers: writing our way to reflective practice'. In Black K., Daiker D. A., Sommers J. and Stygall G. (eds) *New directions in portfolio assessment: reflective practice, critical theory, and large-scale scoring.* Portsmouth, NH: Boynton/Cook Heinemann.

Baxter, A. (1997) *Evaluating your students.* Richmond Publishing.

Beigy, A. and Woodin, J. (1999) *Tandem observation.* Leeds Metropolitan University.

Beigy, A. and Woodin, J. (1999) 'Developing skills in teaching languages'. Part of *Developing excellence in language teaching through the observation of peers.* Leeds Metropolitan University.

Blanche, P. (1988) 'Self-assessment of foreign language skills: implications for teachers and researchers'. *RELC Journal*, 19/1: 75–93.

Burns, A. (1999). *Collaborative action research for English language teachers.* Cambridge University Press.

Buzan, T. and Buzan, B. (1996). *The mind map book: how to use radiant thinking to maximise your brain's untapped potential*. Plume.

Cosh, J. (1999). 'Peer observation: a reflective model'. *ELT Journal*, 53/1.

Edge, J. (1992) *Cooperative development: professional self-development through cooperation with colleagues*. Longman.

Edge, J. (2002) *Continuing cooperative development*. Michigan: Michigan University Press.

Elliot, J. (1991). *Action research for educational change*. Open University Press.

Ellis, G. and Sinclair, B. (1989) *Learning to learn English: a course in learner training*. Cambridge University Press.

Fullerton, H. (1999) 'Observation of teaching'. In Fry, H., Ketteridge, S. and Marshall, S. (eds) *A handbook for teaching and learning in higher education*. Kogan Page.

Lewkowicz, J. A. and Moon, J. (1985) 'Evaluation: a way of involving the learner'. In Alderson, J. C. (ed) *Lancaster Practical Papers in English Language Education, Vol. 6: Evaluation*. Pergamon Press: 45–80.

Makarova, V., and Ryan, S. M. (1997) 'The language teacher through the students' looking glass and what you find there: preliminary results'. *Speech Communication Education*, 10: 12–154.

Naidu, B., Neeraja, K., Ramani, E., Shivakumar, J. and Viswanatha, V. (1992). 'Researching heterogeneity; an account of teacher-initiated research into large classes'. *ELT Journal* 46/3: 252–263.

Parrot, M. (1993). *Tasks for language teachers*. Cambridge University Press.

Politzer, R. L. and McGroarty, M. (1985). 'An exploratory study of learning behaviours and their relationship to gains in linguistic and communicative competence'. *TESOL Quarterly* 19: 103–23.

Russell, A.L. and Cohen, L.M. (1997) 'The reflective colleague in e-mail cyberspace: a means for improving university instruction'. *Computers & Education,* 29(4): 137–145.

Sharp, A. (1990) 'Staff/student participation in course evaluation: a procedure for improving course design'. *English Language Teaching Journal*, 44/2: 132–7.

Tannen, D. (1998). *The argument culture*. Virago.

Weir, C. and Roberts, J. (1994) *Evaluation in ELT*. Blackwell.

Wenden, A. (1991). *Learner strategies for learner autonomy*. Prentice Hall International (UK) Ltd.

Williams, M. and Burden, R. L. (1994) 'The role of evaluation in ELT project design'. *English Language Teaching Journal*, 48/1: 22–27.

Wolf, D. P. (1989). 'Portfolio assessment: sampling student work.' *Educational Leadership*, 46: 35–39.

Self-access to professional development, teaching and learning resources

Please note that the websites quoted below were correct at the time of going to press. If you can't get through, contact CILT (**www.cilt.org.uk**) to find out whether a new website is available.

Chapter 1

ICT/ILT

Throughout this book we have used the term ICT (Information and Communication Technology) when referring to any form of technology (e.g. PCs, interactive whiteboard on the one end of the spectrum, or tape recorders, OHPs and video recorders on the other). These forms of technology are commonly used in other aspects of life and industry, but refer in our case to their application in language teaching and learning. Increasingly the term ILT (Information and Learning Technology) is used to describe any aspect of technology specifically employed for the purpose of teaching and learning.

E-Learning

Another term which is coming to mean 'learning from technology' is e-Learning. When this term was first used, it was generally in the context of on-line learning. E-Learning has now started to be used interchangeably with ICT and ILT, and one factor contributing to this has been the publication in July 2003 of the DfES consultation document *Towards a unified e-Learning strategy*, in which e-Learning is defined as learning from any form of technology, including tapes and videos. 'On-line learning' refers to courses that are delivered electronically, i.e. all course materials plus instructions/tasks are accessible via the Web.

ICT4LT project

A European-funded project, ICT4LT is dedicated to Information and Communications Technology for Language Teachers. A total of sixteen training modules have been completed and are continually updated. Information and training modules are available on-line, on CD-ROM and in printed format. For more information see **www.ict4lt.org/en/**.

COMMUNITEC project

This project is based at the Language Centre at the London School of

Economics. It provides free on-line ICT training for teachers of languages. It was developed in response to the need to train language tutors within the Centre to use the technology available to them and is a good example of what can be done to provide cost-effective on-line training. The on-line materials are freely available and can be used by anyone, although the references are specific to the LSE Language Centre. See **ww.lse.ac.uk/Depts/language/Communitec/HTML/frame.htm**.

TechLearn

Technologies for Learning and Teaching provides advice and support to further and higher education on new and emerging technologies that support learning and teaching. Although not strictly language related, it's a useful resource when deciding on different technologies (write-ups of broadband, video-conferencing, etc). See **www.techlearn.ac.uk**.

Pedagogic training for staff

DELPHI

DELPHI offers a range of on-line subject-specific modules to teachers of any modern foreign language. The DELPHI materials consist of 15 distance-learning modules on different aspects of language teaching. The materials are aimed both at those who are new to the profession and more experienced teachers keen to refresh knowledge and update skills as part of their ongoing professional development. The modular approach means the materials are equally relevant to language teachers working in language departments, language centres and departments of continuing education. Access to all the modules and other areas of the website is completely free of charge to anyone teaching in higher education. **www.delphi.bham.ac.uk**.

Distance learning courses

MAs by distance learning are offered by:

University of Dundee – Certificate/Diploma/Master's degree in Teaching Modern Languages to Adults (TMLA). This is a distance learning Masters programme which is three-year part time. Participants can opt for a one year pg Cert course (phase 1 of the Master's). More information available from: **www.dundee.ac.uk/languagestudies/teachers/tmla.htm**.

Leeds Metropolitan University : **www.lmu.ac.uk/cls/courses/teac mamatdevdist.htm**.

University of Hull MA/Diploma in Language Learning Technology: www.cti.hull.ac.uk/malang.

Independent learning

The higher education community has a Subject Centre for Languages, Linguistics and Area Studies based at the University of Southampton. Its website (**www.lang.ltsn.ac.uk/resources/guidecontents.aspx**) contains information of interest to those in other areas of post-19 education. In *The good practice guide* section, you can find the following articles on supporting independent language learning: 'Supporting independent language learning: development for learners and teachers'; 'Resources for independent language learning: design and use'; 'Integrating independent learning with the curriculum'.

Vark – a guide to learning styles – is an interesting website where you can do an on-line questionnaire to assess your own learning style and find out what kinds of strategies might appeal to different learning styles. See **www.vark-learn.com**.

Chapter 2

DIALANG

This is a diagnostic tool for the general public. It includes tests in five skills (reading, listening, writing, vocabulary and structures), which can be accessed in any one of fourteen European languages. Important aspects of DIALANG are **self-assessment** and **feedback**. See **www.dialang.org**.

Chapter 3

Syllabus design

Syllabuses that have been posted on websites can be helpful in deciding content. Hertfordshire County Council have a particularly good site; you can download ready-made syllabuses (called 'curricula' on this site) at **www.thegrid.org.uk/learning/mfl/teaching/resources/**.

Chapter 4

The European Language Portfolio

The UK European Language Portfolio (ELP) for adults is based on the National Language Standards (NLS) and the Common European Framework. It provides an attractive, portable and motivating way for individual learners to maintain an up-to-date record of their language learning experience and to track their changing levels of performance. For more information see **www.cilt.org.uk/qualifications/elp/adultelp.htm**.

Dedicated teaching sites

The website of CILT, The National Centre for Languages at **www.cilt.org.uk** provides information on government policies with regard to MFL as well as a list of recources and ideas for teaching adults and children.

The following site suggests ways of using ICT in the classroom: **www.vtc.ngfl.gov.uk**.

The site of the Foreign Language Teaching Forum, **www.cortland. ed/flteach**, is packed with useful materials and activity ideas.

The site of the European Commission, **www.europa.eu.int/comm/ education/policies/lang/languages**, is dedicated to promoting European languages.

The following site (also available as a CD-ROM publication, *Web literacy/Culture web*) has been developed within the work of the Council of Europe's European Centre for Modern Languages (ECML) in Graz (Austria): **www.ecml.at/projects/voll/literacy**. In the notes for the CD-ROM, the author describes the resource as 'a training resource specifically for language teachers based on [this] experience – using the web for language teaching'.

Also available on the ECML site, on-line only, are individual dossiers of sites for the teaching and learning of specific languages. The general link is as follows: **www.ecml.at/doccentre/researchdetail.asp?rg=2**, where they are described as 'Commented collections of websites'. The languages in question are: Catalan; Estonian; French (FLE); German; Greek; Hungarian; Italian; Lesser used languages; Polish; Russian; Spanish.

Dedicated learning sites

The BBC's website at **www.bbc.co.uk/languages/** is a comprehensive and easily accessible site. There are on-line activities in all the main European languages, including Portuguese, Gaelic and Welsh, and Asian languages, such as Chinese.

http://languagelab.bh.indiana.edu is the website of Indiana University and offers on-line exercises in a number of languages, including Korean and Hausa. Some languages are better served than others.

www.eleaston.com is another university site with activities for learning Croatian, Latin and Russian.

www.fredriley.org.uk/call provides links to useful resources in the target languages and is especially good on Middle-Eastern languages. This software database was formerly located at the C&IT Centre, University of Hull, as one of the resources of the LTSN (Learning and Teaching Subject Network) Subject Centre for Languages, Linguistics and Area Studies. It is now a free-standing resource, operating as CALL@Hull, with the URL indicated.

www.turkish-center.com is a course provided by Ankara University's Turkish Distance Learning Center, based in the Turkish and Foreign Language Research and Application Centre (TÖMER). It is supported by various on-line facilities, and includes the possibility of accreditation from the university.

The ICT Toolkit – this resource was developed to enable teachers of foreign languages at all levels to create ICT based activities. It provides templates for four activities: hangman, beat-the-clock multiple choice, noughts and crosses, and word search. Because the templates are given, all that is required of the teachers is to input the vocabulary or structures they would like to reinforce in the target and native languages. The computer does the rest! It is envisaged that, with time, a pool of resources will be created that can be shared through the website with other teachers. The Toolkit can be accessed by requesting a user name and password from the administrator directly from the website: **WWW.BCSIP.ORG/PATHFINDER**.

Webquests

Webquests offer a structured approach to information gathering as students use the information that they find to complete a task, often replicating real workplace tasks. To find out more about webquests, visit the following sites:

- www.ardecol.ac-grenoble/fr/english/tice/enwebquests.htm
- www.pzline.com/webquests/design.html

You find some thoughts about webquests at **http://edweb.sdsu.edu/courses/edtec596/about_webquests.html**.

Penpals

Finding penpals or keypals is a fast, authentic and motivating approach to writing in the target language. If you have problems finding keypals, the website **www.stolaf.edu/network/iecc** has pals in a number of countries looking for partners.

Chapter 5

The Languages Ladder – Steps to Success

In the National Languages Strategy the Government sets out its intention to 'introduce a recognition scheme to complement existing qualification frameworks and give people credit for their language skills'. The Languages Ladder is a voluntary recognition scheme, mapped against both the National Qualifications Framework (NQF) and the Common European Framework (CEF). The Ladder is made up of six stages – Breakthrough, Preliminary, Intermediate, Advanced, Proficiency and Master – currently covering fourteen grades of 'steps'. The system of grades has been devised with 'can do' statements for each of the four skills – Listening, Speaking, Reading and Writing – each of which can be assessed discretely. The Languages Ladder will allow learners to progress in one or more skills and also offers the opportunity for people to assess their own levels of language competence. Each stage is externally assessed, the 'can do' statements within each stage can be used for formative assessment and can be endorsed by the teacher/tutor.

For more information, and a timetable for the development of the scheme, go to **www.dfes.gov.uk/languages/DSP_languagesladder.cfm**.

Chapter 6

Organisations that can help in preparing for inspection

It would be impossible to provide a complete picture of all the organisations who can support the development of a coherent policy for furthering continuing professional development and preparing for outside evaluation. However, the following list is a good start:

Adult Learning Inspectorate

The site contains the full text of key ALI documents and press releases, plus Training Standards Council inspection reports. **www.ali.gov.uk**.

Association of Colleges

There is interesting information on the Raising Quality and Achievement (RQA) project: **www.aoc.co.uk**.

CILT, the National Centre for Languages

There is a great deal of useful information on this site **www.cilt.org.uk**.

Council for Learning Resources in Colleges

The guidelines to inspection (for colleges) are useful. **www.colric.org.uk**.

FE Resources for Learning (FERL)

Those teachers interested in the effective use of Information Learning Technology (ILT) in language teaching may find this site informative. **http://ferl.becta.org.uk.**

Further Education National Training Organisation

This organisation is responsible for the development, quality assurance and promotion of national standards for the further education sector. There is useful information on teaching and supporting learning **www.fento.org**.

Learning Skills Council

This organisation supports further education and sixth form colleges, and representatives of community groups, to understand, define and then meet training and education needs. **www.lsc.gov.uk**.

National Information and Learning Technologies Association

The site has information for those in adult learning who are interested in the development, use and exploitation of ILT. **www.nilta.org.uk**.

National Institute of Adult Continuing Education

The role of the National Institute of Adult Continuing Education (NIACE) is to promote the study and general advancement of adult continuing education. **www.niace.org.uk**.

Office for Standards in Education

Ofsted is a non-ministerial government department whose main aim is to help improve the quality and standards of education through independent inspection and regulation. **www.ofsted.gov.uk**.

TeacherNet

Useful information about continued professional development of teachers and trainers. **www.teachernet.gov.uk/Professional_ Development/opportunities/p16staffquals**.

The contributors

Dr Susan Ainslie is Head of Continuing Professional Development at Edge Hill College of Higher Education in Lancashire, where she is responsible for professional development courses for teachers and other professionals working in education. Before then she was Head of Languages at Edge Hill where she set up and led the PGCE in Modern Foregein Languages in French, German, Spanish and Urdu. She also has extensive experience of teaching in adult, further and secondary education and has written articles and books with a main focus on differentiation and assessment. She is an Associate Inspector for the Adult Learning Inspectorate.

Fran Beaton has worked in Adult, Community and Higher Education for over twenty years as a teacher and teacher trainer. For the last nine years she has been Programme Co-ordinator of the Languages and Language Studies programme at Goldsmiths College, London, and has also been designing and teaching a specialist teacher training course for the Diplomatic Service Language Centre at the Foreign Office. She has recently taken up a new post as Academic Staff Developer in the University of Kent Unit for the Enhancement of Learning and Teaching.

Fiona Copland has taught English in Nigeria, Hong Kong, Japan and UK. She is currently Training Coordinator at Brasshouse Language Centre, where she runs pre- and in-service courses for teachers of English and teachers of Modern Foreign Languages. She is also the Coordinator of the MA ED (TEFL) in the School of Education at Birmingham University.

Dr Henriette Harnisch has been a teacher and curriculum manager in AE and FE for some 14 years. During this time she has been involved in designing and delivering a range of CPD and teacher training courses throughout the UK. She has been responsible for the CILT FE networks in the Midlands, the North West, the South West and London and, until 2003, was Head of MFL at the Brasshouse Language Centre in Birmingham. She is currently Regional Director for Languages in the Black Country, a role that evolved from her heading up the 14–19 Networks for Excellence Pathfinder project in the region.

Dr Steve Mann has worked as a language teacher in Europe and S E Asia. His current teacher development role at Aston University allows him to work with language teachers in many countries. He is particularly interested in developing action research projects which help improve the experience of language learners.

Alan Moys spent his whole career in the field of languages education, with teaching experience in schools, further education and teacher training. He also served as an education adviser in Derbyshire before moving to CILT as Deputy Director and then as Director. After his 'retirement' in 1992 he continued his work as a writer and a schools inspector, becoming Chairman and then President of the National Association of Language Advisers (NALA). At the invitation of the Nuffield Foundation, he returned to full-time engagement from 1998 to 2000 as Secretary of the Nuffield Languages Inquiry.

Linda Parker began her career teaching French in secondary schools, then worked for many years in both higher and adult education. More recently she has been Head of Information and Resources at CILT, a Principal Lecturer at the Nottingham Trent University and is currently Director of the Association for Language Learning.

Pauline Swanton is a Senior Manager at Leicester Adult Education College where she oversees the running of a diverse programme for learners that includes a significant languages provision. She advises CILT, the National Centre for Languages, on adult education matters. A long career in adult education has encompassed teaching French and English, management and consultancy on issues for older learners and language matters for a number of agencies.